The LAST TROLLEY OUT

The LAST TROLLEY OUT

Morris Venden

THE LAST TROLLEY OUT—HOW *NOT* TO PREPARE FOR THE END!

Senior Editor: Bill Morelan • Copy Editor: Mary Alice Hill • Cover Illustration: Todd Williams • Cover Design: MOE Studio • Graphics: Daniel Potter

Vintage Publications • Post Office Box 147 • Gentry, AR 72734

Vintage Publications is a division of The Concerned Group, Inc.
ISBN #0-936785-92-6

Dedicated to the Lord Jesus,
my best friend!

Contents

Foreword

The purpose of this book is to share the exciting good news that you don't have to be on "the last trolley out" when Jesus comes! In fact, we'll look at God's resources for *not* being on that trolley.

For some time now, I've resisted the Christian community's obsessive interest in last day events—perhaps because of an overdose of that theme while growing up on the sawdust trail. But a deeper concern has caused my resistance to continue. It's the idea that if I know the *very final events*, I can catch "the last trolley out."

Hoping to catch "the last trolley out" can be based on several bad reasons. One, for example, is that I can't keep my act together any longer than that! Another might be that I want to have all the "fun" the world has to offer for as long as possible, then pull a squeeze play through the city gates into the heavenly country.

This mentality is repulsive to anyone who really understands what the cross of Jesus means to the genuine Christian. If I don't respond to the love of God—whether He comes back tomorrow, or ten thousand years from now—I won't be on *any* trolley. In other words, those hoping to get on the *last* trolley have already *missed* the trolley!

I know that some have said, "I don't care if I'm the last one through the gates, as long as I'm there." But while this may sound humble and pious, God has a much better plan! He has assured each one of us an *abundant* entrance into His kingdom.

And so, this book is dedicated to those who are more excited about seeing Jesus, than memorizing the order of last day events so they can barely slip through.

—Morris Venden
Riverside, California, 1995

Chapter One

Faith in the CRISIS

You know the story. A wise man and a wise woman (and a wise boy and girl) built their house upon the rock. The foolish man and the foolish woman (and the foolish boy and girl) built their house upon the sand. The wind blew and the floods came and the house on the rock stood firm. But the house on the sand had a great fall!

As we begin to study the final events of this world's history, let's focus for a few moments on this little parable that Jesus told at the end of the sermon on the mount. You'll find it in Matthew, chapter seven. It's short and to the point, but carries with it some heavy principles. Here Jesus gives us a warning (I suppose, in one sense, we might call it a dish of vegetarian hell) to consider the ominous issues of the end time, and whether we are ready or not.

Some people have been scared into the church. It's doubtful, however, whether anyone will ever be scared into the kingdom of heaven. But maybe this is as close as we're going to get to Jesus warning us about some things that are really frightening:

"'Therefore everyone who hears these words of mine and puts them into practice is like a wise man who built his house on the rock. The rain came down, the streams rose, and the winds blew and beat against that house; yet it did not fall, because it had its foundation on the rock. But everyone who hears these words of mine and does not put them into practice is like a foolish man who built his house on sand. The rain came down, the streams rose, and the winds blew and beat against that house, and it fell with a great crash.' When Jesus had finished saying these things, the crowds were amazed at his teaching, because he taught as one who had authority, and not as their teachers of the law." (Matthew 7:24-29)

Interpreting the Parable

So what are these sayings of His? They must be contained in the Sermon on the Mount. More specifically, they must have come before this parable, since He started it with, "Therefore"—referring to His teachings that went before.

What is the house? What is the rock? What is the sand? If we let Scripture interpret itself, we discover that the Bible calls *us* buildings of God. We are likened, as individuals, to a building. "Now we know that if the earthly tent we live in is destroyed, we have a building from God, an eternal house in heaven, not built by human hands." (2 Corinthians 5:1) So, the house analogy that's used in Scripture refers to us.

But what are *we* standing on? What is *our* dependence? What is our foundation? And what is the rock and the sand?

Again, if we let the Bible interpret itself, the rock becomes quite clear. The rock is a person—Christ Jesus. Perhaps you've read about the mud and metal image of Daniel two. The rock that was cut out of the mountain without hands and smote the great image represented Jesus and His kingdom. The rock is also spoken of as the Stone the builders rejected, and it became the head of the corner.

The New Testament makes it clear that if we fall on this Rock we're going to be broken. Now that doesn't sound very pleasant. It means surrender—coming to the end of our own resources and learning to depend on the *real* foundation. But if the rock falls on us (as in the days of Daniel and his mud and metal image) it will grind us to powder! So there are only two options. Don't you like the first one better? To fall on the rock, even though we're going to be broken?

Now what about sand? Well, that speaks for itself, too. We can't very well depend on shifting sand for a foundation. I'm reminded of something I read about those defeated in life. Christians who are trying to do better in their own strength, soon discover that their "promises and resolutions are like ropes of sand". People who've tried to develop righteousness by promise, righteousness by resolution, righteousness by determination or backbone—regardless of how strong they are—still find their efforts to be sand. In Christ's day, the religious leaders gave pretty good evidence that in the end they didn't have much foundation. They were depending upon themselves, and the Bible says that whoever trusts in himself is a fool. This gets tricky, because if I depend upon myself (and I'm a strong person), I can fool myself into thinking that I *have* a foundation. But when the big winds blow, no one will go through on self-discipline or backbone. No self-sufficient person will be able to make it through that kind of crisis.

When the Big Wind Blows

Now in the Christian life, we can develop something we might call "spiritual schizophrenia"—often demonstrated in the days of yore. There are people, like Judas, who looked just as good (maybe even better) than the other disciples. And nobody knew what they were really like until the big crisis in their life. Then we have people like

Peter who say, "Look, Lord, you can count on me! Everyone else is going to leave you, but not me. I'll hang in there!" But only a short time later he found out what he was really like. The big wind blew and his true self was revealed.

Consider two trees in the forest. They both look the same until the big winds come and one of them gives evidence that it is rotten on the inside. It crashes to the ground while the other stands straight and tall. It all happens in that moment of crisis.

Sometimes we think that we can deal with crises. We look around at people who crumble and think, "Well, I wouldn't behave like that. I can stand tall through the big winds." But then, to our dismay, we discover the truth. We think we can brave the storms on a thousand seas, but we drown to death in the bathtub! It's a cruel revelation.

Some people are sure they'd never do anything stupid like trying to rescue the frying pan from a burning house. But our family was in a fire once. Did we rescue the important papers and documents? No, we managed to save a bunch of coat hangers! How foolish can you get? You never *really* know what you'll do until the big winds blow.

Setting the Stage

Those who study behavioral science tell us that every decision made in a crisis is premeditated. What does that mean? It means everything that's gone before has set me up for what I'm going to do when a crisis comes. My background, my environment, my temperament, my personality, the billions of pieces of data I've put into my head—everything predetermines my behavior *before* the big winds blow.

I have a friend who entered the Korean war as a conscientious objector. He would not use a weapon. He would only help with medical needs. But as he first stepped foot on the shores of Korea, his stretcher-mate was shot down on the beach. My conscientious objector friend grabbed the nearest rifle, and shot to kill the rest of the Korean war. Then he came home burdened with guilt. He was appalled to find out, when the crisis hit, who he really was.

On the other hand, the military has taken careful surveys to discover how many of those trained to line up their sights and kill the enemy, actually performed as expected in real-life situations. They found out it was only twelve percent. Amazing! When it came right down to the wire and they had to zero in on someone's head or heart, they raised their rifles and shot the birds, or the clouds, or the trees. Evidently there are a lot more conscientious objectors than we thought there were. I like that! The crises revealed that what they did was really premeditated. So, perhaps the principle is not too far off.

Last Minute Changes?

Now in this story Jesus told about the rock and the sand, there's one major point we need to zero in on: *The house does not change foundations in the storm!* If we have time, we might change afterwards, but we will *never* change when the crisis hits. All the big wind does is reveal who or what we already are. That's all. This shows how ridiculous it is to think we're going to get on the last trolley out when the final big winds begin to blow. It just won't happen.

In the first place, the whole "last trolley" mentality is a slap in the face of Jesus who suffered the cross for me. My response to Him should not be based on any panic, or crisis, or big winds that blow.

In the second place, Jesus taught that it just doesn't happen that way. He made this very clear in the story of the rock and the sand. A crisis doesn't *change* us—it only reveals what we already are.

And this is true for small winds as well as big ones. If I get hit with pain or tragedy or sorrow or separation now, it's a very real opportunity to find out what really makes me tick and how deep I really go.

There's something else they tell us about these crises that come when the winds blow. Not only do we find out where we really are, but we increase momentum, and continue faster in the direction we're already going! It happens when you climb a mountain. If you're walking up a mountain and you fall, when you get up again, you'll be a few steps higher than when you fell. But if you're going downhill and you fall, when you get up again you'll be several steps *below* where you fell.

Peter stands straight and tall and says, "Lord, I will not deny you." (Major problem, self-sufficiency) But then when the crisis hits (by the fire, with the maiden pointing her finger at him) Peter not only denies Jesus, but the momentum increases as he denies with curses and swearing. It was a terrible night for Peter—but it was a real opportunity for him to learn how solid his foundation really wasn't.

Regarding "Deathbed Experiences"

Now if these principles concerning crises are true, this brings into serious question so-called deathbed repentances. I hesitate to bring this up because I like to hold on to the hope that loved ones or friends that I have known, who apparently came to God at the last moment, really *did* come to God. I don't want to explode any hopes or open up any old wounds. But the principle in this parable makes it very clear that counting on "deathbed repentance" could be quite dangerous.

But, people say, "What about the thief on the cross?" Well, we don't really know that much about the thief on the cross. He could have heard the Gospel, could have been baptized by John, could have later fallen into bad company.

If people don't respond to the love of God *before* they're facing death, then what, pray tell, is going to make them respond any more when they barely have enough blood pumping across their cerebrum to allow them to think clearly?

As I pondered this, I remembered the case of the desperate man who called for me from the hospital. It was early in my experience, and I had the idea that God answers the prayers of the perfect, but He can't do much for the imperfect. Somewhere at home, school, or church, I'd picked up this mistaken idea that you had to be about ready for translation before you could ask God for special favors. Then I met this man for the first time in the hospital. He'd had a terrible heart attack. He could barely breathe. He gasped to me, "Please, I've treated God badly. I've really treated God shabbily. But, would you pray for me that I can come up in the right resurrection?"

Well, let's be so presumptuous as to analyze this situation for a moment. Do we have here a response to the cross, a sincere response to the love of God? It sounds like panic to me! He studied about these things as a child. He remembered about the two resurrections. And now he's afraid he's going to come up in the wrong one. It reminded me of an experience my marine friend (from college days) had in Korea. In the middle of the night, an unexpected communist machine gunner was mowing down his company from the opposite hill. He found himself about to die at any moment on the side of a mountain. My friend prayed the same prayer, "God, I don't have any time. Just help me come up in the right resurrection." Sheer panic! Concern for himself and his chances for eternity.

Well, at the hospital bed, I prayed for the man to come up in the right resurrection. There were no elders. There was no oil. But this man was healed! He walked out of that hospital with a heart as good as anyone. And I just couldn't figure it out.

Then it began to slowly dawn on me. Couldn't a loving God be kind enough to give someone under panic a chance to respond instead to the cross and the love of Jesus? Might He not be willing to allow them to discover for themselves if it was just a fear-induced reaction, or whether they would *really* respond to the good news of the Gospel? It began to come together and to make some sense.

I'd like to hold out, as much as possible, for deathbed "repentances", but we need to remember what "repentance" really is.

Understanding Repentance

We often sorrow because our evil deeds bring us unpleasant consequences. But this is *not* true repentance. Real sorrow for sin is the result of the working of the Holy Spirit. The Spirit reveals the ingratitude of the heart that has slighted and grieved the Savior, and brings us in contrition to the foot of the cross. Jesus is wounded afresh by our every sin, and as we look upon Him whom we have pierced, we mourn for the sins that have brought anguish to Him. Such mourning will lead us to renounce sin.

After all, if I'm not won by the love of Jesus, no amount of anything else (including panic) will ever bring me to salvation. When we talk about last-minute or deathbed repentance, we must remember what true repentance is all about: False repentance is being sorry I'm in trouble. Genuine repentance is being sorry I've broken the heart of my best friend.

And it's a little late to get acquainted with your best friend when you're consumed by panic!

So, if I have any idea that I'm going to memorize the charts and know all of the last day events in order (so I can get on the last trolley out), I'd better remember this simple warning by Jesus: We do not change foundations when the big winds blow. We just don't do it.

About Trials and Testing

There's an interesting, almost humorous text, found in Jeremiah the twelfth chapter, verse five. "If you have raced with men on foot and they have worn you out, how can you compete with horses? If you stumble in safe country, how will you manage in the flooding of the Jordan?"

Don't try to run with the horses if you can't keep up with the footmen. Don't try to make it through times of stress, if you can't make it in times of peace. If you're uncomfortable jumping off the back steps, don't take up skydiving. If you're not relaxed in the bathtub, don't go in for scuba diving. If you don't know what six times nine is, don't register for trigonometry. And if you can't make it when small winds blow, don't think you're going to make it when the big winds come.

Now, I find it very interesting that God, in His infinite love, will allow the small winds to blow while there's still time to change after we find out what makes us tick. Remember, we don't change in the crisis (although we might change after the crisis, if there's time.)

Some of these small winds don't look very small. Facing terminal illness doesn't look small. Having a handicapped child doesn't look very small. Experiencing a sudden accident doesn't look very small. But these bumps and bruises that come from living on the wrong planet can actually help us grow.

James said it rather clearly: "Consider it pure joy, my brothers, whenever you face trials of many kinds..." (Why different kinds of temptations? Because different trials and stresses and temptations help us understand which way we're going!) "...because you know that the testing of your faith develops perseverance. Perseverance must finish its work so that you may be mature and complete, not lacking anything." (James 1: 2-4)

One of these days (according to the eighth chapter of Amos) there are apparently going to be millions of people running from sea to sea and coast to coast seeking the word of the Lord—and they can't find it! It will be panic city, panic country, panic world, because they're looking for something they thought they could get at the last minute, and it just doesn't happen that way! So, I should thank God for whatever stress or strain that comes to help me understand where I am now. That way, when the final wind blows (and there's no chance to change after) I'll have done my homework, listened to His sayings, and responded to His love. Painful—but it makes sense.

Doing God's Will

There are two of Jesus' sayings that come just before this little parable. They have to do with knowing if I'm for real. The first is found in Matthew 7:21: "Not everyone who says to me, 'Lord, Lord,' will enter the kingdom of heaven, but only he who does the will of my Father who is in heaven." So the first way to know whether we're doing God's will has to do with obedience.

But that can be tricky. It's been tricky since the days of Jesus and before, because some strong people can fake obedience. And they did! There were schizophrenics in the days of Jesus. They were great on church going and rule keeping and family worship and tithe paying—but they had murder in their hearts. They could fake it on the outside (as Jesus pointed out in Matthew 23), but they were rotten on the inside. Apparently this kind of "doing the will of God" is not what Jesus had in mind.

The second saying helps clear this up. It's found in Matthew 7:23: "Then I will tell them plainly, 'I never knew you. Away from me, you evildoers!'" The problem of those who are lost is that they never knew Jesus. Here Jesus makes it clear that knowing Him is the bottom line. A relationship with Him brings obedience because I know Him and love Him. I don't obey on my own—that's impossible. The only *genuine* "doing of the will of God" comes as the result of knowing Him. And when we know Him, as it is our privilege to know Him, our life will be a life of obedience. So, there you have it— faith, resulting in works.

The Relationship of Faith and Works

Now at this point, I've heard people say, "That's it. You've got to have faith and works in order to be saved." Or, as someone once said to me, "Faith and works are like two oars. You use both of them to row your way across the sea of life to the heavenly country."

And I said, "No way!" We are saved *only* by faith—works are simply the result of that faith.

Yes, faith and works could be compared to two oars when it comes to their *importance.* But obedience is the *result* (or proof) of faith. They are equally important, but it's vital that we understand that one is the *cause* of the other.

In the setting of this parable, how do we build on the rock? Only by getting to know Jesus. And this will result in a changed life. Then when those big winds begin to blow, they will reveal who we really are—a true friend of Jesus!

The BIG Test

I have a favorite war story about the training camps in England. English and American soldiers were trained for the highly dangerous business of espionage and counter espionage. They went through a training program so rigorous that before long it was apparent the commanders were actually trying to change their identity. American and English soldiers were "becoming Germans." They taught them the German language. They taught them German phrases. They taught them German thinking. They fed them German black bread. They dressed them in German uniforms.

Then came the big test. They went out on a bivouac and were on a grueling march until late at night . Finally, dead tired, they were allowed to crumple into their pup tents exhausted. In the middle of the night, they were suddenly awakened with a bright light in their eyes and someone shouting at them, "Who are you?" This was the crucial moment. If they responded: "I'm Henry Smith." "Where are you from?" "Canada." "Where are you going?" "I'm going home to Mamma."—it wasn't long until they were back home with Mamma. But if, with the bright lights in their eyes, they shouted back, "Mine namen isht Heinrique Schmidt." "Where are your from?" "Hamburg." "Where are you going?" "Frankfurt."—it wasn't long before they were headed for Hamburg or Frankfurt.

The FINAL Test

One of these days, the spotlight of final great events will shine in our faces. We'll wake up, as though from a deep sleep, with someone shouting, "Who are you?" If we've listened to these sayings of Jesus, then we can respond, "I am a follower of Jesus." "Where are you from?" "I'm a stranger and pilgrim on the earth." "Where are you going?" "I'm going to a city which hath foundations, whose builder and maker is God." Then we will be grateful for the blessing of having had some small winds in order to go through the big one.

Chapter Two

How To Be READY

Some years ago, a new song was introduced on the Christian circuit. I don't know how far it went in the evangelical world, but it was a song called "Are you ready for Jesus to come?" It achieved a great degree of popularity. I still know the words from hearing it sung as a solo. I even sang the song myself. But, I'm kind of glad that song went away.

"Are you ready for Jesus to come?" (Not a bad question, but then came the answers.) "Are you faithful in *all* that you do?" (Ouch!) "Have you fought a good fight? Have you stood for the right?" "Have others seen Jesus in you?" (Ouch again!)

Now, please don't get me wrong. I'm in favor of being faithful in all that we do, and standing for the right—and I hope that others can see Jesus in me. But not *as the basis* for getting ready for Jesus to come! The Christian world has had its share of behavior-centered focusing. I suppose this song reflects how many of us have legalistically thought "we've got to get faithful in all that we do in order to be ready for Jesus to come—so we'd better start working on it!"

I've heard it more than once: "Let's get ready for Jesus to come." But, there's a better way to approach this. The phrase "getting ready" seems to reflect behavior-centered thinking. There's a big difference between *getting* ready and *being* ready.

Jesus made it very clear that we don't know the day or the hour of His coming. In fact, He said *no one* knew it but His Father only. Now that's rather exclusive! And it can leave us a little frustrated. When we have guests for dinner and we know exactly when they're coming, it helps with the stress. (If we didn't know exactly *when* they were coming—maybe sometime this month—it could be really stressful!) If we know they're coming at six o'clock, we can plan on it. We can prepare. We can be ready even if they say, "sixish" because at least that's within the hour. (Knowing when they plan to leave kind of helps too, because many of us find it hard to be nicer than we really are for too long a time.)

But, Jesus leaves the day and the hour hanging. Obviously we're going to have to approach this problem from a different direction than the usual form of "getting ready", in order to have peace—and in order to be able to look forward to it!

Ready for Jesus

Let's try to get a handle on what it means to "be ready" for Jesus to come. I want to get this resolved early in this book on last events, because once we get this settled we can approach (with peace) the rest of the items—big times of trouble, political and world crises, etc.

To begin with, I'd like to suggest that the *more* mature we are as Christians, the *less* concerned we're going to be with this topic!

Moses, one of history's most mature Christians (after the bumps and bruises of his earlier experiences), was willing to forgo his own eternal life for the sake of others. In his discussion with God about saving two million garlic-smelling illiterates from Egypt, he put his own eternal destiny into the balance. (Exodus 32:31,32) In the same way, the mature Christian is much more concerned about *others* being ready, than whether or not *he's* going to make it.

There's another reason we don't want to spend forever on this topic. The devil often leads many conscientious Christians (who sincerely desire to live for God) to dwell on their own imperfections and weaknesses. And by thus separating them from Christ, he hopes to gain the victory. We should never make ourselves the center, and indulge in anxiety and fear as to whether we shall be saved. All this turns the soul away from the source of our strength.

In other words, if we spend all of our time talking about how to be ready for Jesus to come, that in itself could become a contributing factor toward *not* being ready! We should commit the keeping of our souls to God, and let self be lost in Him. We can put away all doubt. We can dismiss our fears and rest in Jesus. He is able to keep that which we have committed to Him. If we leave ourselves in His hands, He will bring us off "more than conquerors through Him that has loved us."

Committed to Him

So what are the things we *can* do? First, commit the keeping of your soul to God. That's a significant word for these days. The only way *anyone* can have security is to have commitment! Second, talk and think of Jesus. As we consider last day events, we must continue to keep Jesus as the center of our focus. And third, leave yourself in His hands. That means that we've already come into His presence—and now we can stay with Him.

As we said earlier concerning the time when Jesus said He would come again, no one knows the day or the hour. He made it very clear that this was the plight of the ten bridesmaids. It was no problem for five of them. But in Matthew 25, where He spoke of this, there were five foolish bridesmaids who had forgotten to check their oil. And while they were out looking for oil at midnight, the bridegroom came. So, He said in the conclusion of this story, "Watch!"

Watch for what? Whether "I am faithful in all that I do," or whether I know Him and am in His hands? There's a crucial difference!

Let's look at some significant verses in Scripture on this point. First, 2 Timothy 1:11,12. Here we have the Apostle Paul talking about being called as an apostle, a teacher, and a preacher—and how he has suffered many things, but wasn't ashamed. Then he says, "...because I know whom I have believed, and am convinced that he is able to guard what I have entrusted to him for that day."

People have written songs about this verse. In fact, there's one that used to be a favorite, "I know not why God's wondrous grace, to me He hath made known. Nor why, unworthy, Christ in love redeemed me for his own. But I know whom I have believe-ed..." (That's how the song went—probably why it died. So, let's change it to "I know whom I have believed *in.")* "...and am persuaded that He is able to keep that which I've committed, unto Him against that day." Again, the idea is that of *commitment* to the one with whom I am having a trusting relationship—not just today but until "that day" (referring to the coming of Christ).

Several years ago, my brother and I stood in the Mamertine dungeon by the Tiber River in Rome. It was a rainy afternoon, and we were alone there. We read the book of 2 Timothy, which was written in that place. We saw the hole down through which they threw the Apostle Paul for his last days. We saw the opening to the underground passage where they led him to the beheader's block.

And we could almost see Paul, looking up toward heaven. We could almost read his mind as the beheader's ax fell: "For I am...being poured out like a drink offering, and the time has come for my departure. I have fought the good fight, I have finished the race, I have kept the faith. Now there is in store for me a crown of righteousness, which the Lord, the righteous Judge, will award to me on that day..." (2 Timothy 6-8) And the very next instant, as far as Paul is concerned, he sees "that day"—the day of Jesus coming.

Whether you and I live or die, we will see Jesus come. And the significant question is, "Do I know whom I have believed in? Have I committed to Him, like the faithful of all ages?"

Abiding in Him

There's another text on this topic found in 1 John 2:28. This text is directed at the children. So all you little children (up to age ninety) please consider this verse: "And now, dear children, abide in him, so that when He appears we may be confident and unashamed before him at his coming." What's the clue here? What's the solution for being ready? *Abiding* in Him! But what does that mean? To abide means to stay—to *stay* with Him.

So there's something equally as important as *coming* to Him. It's *staying* with Him. And if we do, we will not be ashamed at His coming. That means that if I want to know I'm ready for His coming today, then I need an *abiding relationship* with Him.

Are you in a saving relationship with Christ? If you are, then you're ready for His coming right now! You can know this. He offers you this assurance.

There's one other text that surprised me when I first got to it. It's in the setting of the raising of Lazarus. "...whoever lives and believes in me will never die." (John 11:26) Jesus said, if you live in a relationship with Him, and believe in Him, you'll never die!

What does that mean? Well, in this setting, it means you might sleep like Lazarus did, but you'll never die. Isn't that good news?

Think what it would be like if Jesus came to you, as though you were the only person in the world, and He smiled at you with love in His eyes and said, "You will never die." Really? That's right! You might sleep, but you'll never die. As long as you believe in Him, as long as you live in Him, you will never die. Why? Because you're living in a relationship with Him. That's why you're not ashamed when He comes. You *trust* Jesus—not just to begin with, but through every day of your Christian life. That's the big "R" for the Christian, an abiding *relationship* with Christ.

Victory Through Him

I thought about some other things we could consider concerning how to be certain. What about the new birth? We need to make sure we're converted, don't we? John 3 says no one can see the kingdom of God unless they're born again. But, wait a minute. You can't convert yourself, and nobody can convert anyone else. This is totally God's department—and He knows the timetable for each individual. So, let's talk about something that we can have a part in.

"But wait!" you say. "Isn't there anything we can do about conversion?" Well, you can place yourself in the atmosphere where it happens. You can even pray for it. But remember, conversion is totally God's work.

In an attempt to get more tangible, people often slip back into the old "Are you ready for Jesus to come?" mentality. They work hard on obeying and overcoming and being victorious because "...he who overcomes will...be dressed in white. I will never blot out his name from the book of life..." (Revelation 3:5.) This approach focuses on obedience and victory and how to overcome. And there are whole ministries today that have been built in this direction—lifting up the standard for obedience.

It's a big surprise for some of us to discover that victory is totally God's department—that obedience is not something we achieve, not something we work on. Overcoming is not something we grit our teeth and try hard to do. It is a gift. A gift that comes from Jesus.

Hebrews 13:20,21 says it well: "Now the God of peace, that brought again from the dead our Lord Jesus...make you perfect in every good work to do His will, working in you that which is well pleasing in His sight..." (KJV) Are we supposed to make ourselves perfect? No! "The God of peace" makes us perfect. How perfect? "In every good work." What does that include? "To do His will"—which means obeying His commandments. But how does that happen? Through God "working in you that which is well pleasing in His sight."

And so, the whole work of sanctification (of being changed into His likeness, being transformed by grace) is His work. It's God's department, not mine. That's a big surprise to some of us who've been trying so hard to produce righteousness by resolution, righteousness by backbone, and righteousness by grit and determination—to discover that it's *His* work we've been trying to do.

So there's no point in talking about becoming perfect as the basis of our assurance. The basis of knowing that we're ready for Jesus to come is in choosing to have a continuing daily saving relationship with Him. That's where *we* enter into the picture.

Only Half of the Gospel

Now a word of caution. There's a popular theology that's jumped into many churches. Maybe you're familiar with it. It basically says,

"Hey, quit trying to work on your problems. Don't get discouraged over your failures. We're all human. We're all going to make mistakes. In fact, we sin a thousand times a day, and we'll just keep on sinning until Jesus comes. That's why the cross is so beautiful. Let's focus on the cross. Jesus paid it all. He did it all. And we are such desperate sinners that our only hope is in the cross."

Now on the surface, that theology sounds pretty good—but it's only one half of the Gospel! Thousands of people flock to it because they believe the preacher. And that's never been safe for anyone to do! (Listen to the preacher, but don't believe anything he says until you check it out for yourself!)

With this theology, comes the idea that trying to focus on what's happening in our lives is too subjective. "We want," they say, "an objective gospel. Let's get the focus away from us and onto the cross, just the cross. That's all."

This has led some of us to take a second look, with this conclusion: *There's no such thing as salvation by grace*! Now that could run a Gospel preacher out of town in a hurry, couldn't it? But, let me say it again—there is no such thing as salvation by grace. Ephesians 2 says: "For by grace are ye saved through faith; and that not of yourselves, it is the gift of God." (verses 8,9) So even faith is a gift.

The minute you add *faith* to grace, you involve two parties—one trusting the other. You can't leave out the subjective! There's no such thing as "believe the Gospel and focus only on the cross". The cross waves its friendly arms toward people to *respond,* to enter into fellowship with the One who came to save us. Yet God doesn't intend to save us against our will. He's persistent, but He's not pushy. It's up to us to decide whether we enter into this saving faith relationship.

Another problem with this theology is that it carries with it the need to get rid of the judgment. If you're using this view to be certain about Jesus coming, you can't have a scary judgment with every work coming into review. So, some people throw the judgment out. Then they get nervous about the Bible teachings concerning obedience, victory, and overcoming. So they have to get rid of these as well.

A lot of people go for this theology because they're looking for some kind of readiness for Jesus' coming that doesn't involve too much time, effort, or concern on their part. They find death to self (on a daily basis) a rather tiring and wearisome task. There are those who would rather spend half a day watching football than half an hour reading the Bible; those more devoted to the stock market than to their prayer life; those who'd rather spend hours listening to a "ghetto blaster" than thinking of eternal things. They're all looking for an easier way to be sure about Jesus' coming. And so, even in the church, we have those who say, "Isn't there an easier way? Can't I just have my 'text for the day' with my hand on the door knob? Do I *really* need to have quality time alone with Jesus? Do I really need to spend time one-on-one with God?" And they go for the easier way.

Another "easier" method that some people have explored is righteousness by feeling. Get your emotions pumped up every week and that will get you feeling saved and safe and ready for Jesus to come. These people are not satisfied with a meeting unless they have a powerful and happy time. They work to generate excitement and feeling. But the influence of such meetings is not beneficial. When the happy flight of feeling is gone, they sink lower than before because their happiness did not come from the right source. (You can't rely on emotions in a human marriage *or* in a marriage with Christ. There has to be something deeper than just feelings.)

The most profitable meetings for spiritual advancement are those characterized by deep searching of the heart—each person present seeking to know himself better, and in earnest, deep humility, seeking to learn more of Christ. For the more we learn of Christ, the more we want Him—and the deeper our fellowship with Him!

Two Kinds of Legalists

Then there are the legalists. Have you ever considered that there's more than one kind? One new form is the "liberal legalist". These are people who say, "I'm tired of the rules and regulations of the church that tell me what I can and can't do! I want to go where I please, and act as I choose. I'm done with all that legalism stuff. I'm going to settle for love, forgiveness, and acceptance." But as liberal as they seem, they're still legalists. Their attention is still on the rules and the regulations and the standards of the church—but from the other side of the behavioral coin.

The old-time legalists found their security in rigidly upholding the rules and regulations and standards of the church. But the liberal legalists look for security in the rules and regulations and standards of the church that they abandon. "I'm not a legalist", they say. "I act as I choose, go where I want, and do what I please because of the cross".

Now that's a slap in the face of Jesus, because the cross of Christ *changes* us! The person who enters into an abiding, saving relationship with Jesus is not going to drag God down to his level. He's going to be changed. But remember, his hope of eternal life is not *based* on this change. That's the *result* of his hope of eternal life. And the blessed assurance that we can have in fellowship with Christ leaves us "not ashamed at His coming". If we know Him today, we'll know Him when He comes—and He will know us as well!

Behavior vs. Relationship

"Well," you say. "If the whole thing hinges on a saving relationship with Christ, what about relationship failure? Isn't it possible to have a failure in a relationship just like we've had behavior failure?"

Of course. Jesus said it in Matthew 24:12,13 "Because of the increase of wickedness, the love of most will grow cold, but he who stands firm to the end will be saved." So, there's the challenge of enduring to the end, even in terms of a loving relationship.

How can you know when a relationship is growing thin? There's less talking, less listening, and less going places and doing things together. Can you notice when that's happening? Sure. Can you know when you're reading your Bible less, enjoying it less, and praying less? Of course! Can you know if you've lost the joy of witnessing and service for Christ? Yes! So what can you do about it?

First, go to your knees and tell God you've got a problem. Next, join up with a small group of fellow travelers toward the heavenly country, where you can gain encouragement and compare notes on what's helping others. If your eyes are open, you'll know when you're on the relationship failure track. Then if you're serious concerning the things of eternity, you can renew your relationship with Jesus.

Did the disciples experience behavior problems? They sure did! Enter the upper room with the disciples. Sing to them, "Are you ready for Jesus to come." (They're bickering and arguing about who's going to be the greatest.) Sing the next stanza, "Are you faithful in *all* that you do?" (That would put them under the table at the last supper.) "Have you fought a good fight? Have you stood for the right? Have others seen Jesus in you?" (This is the group that said "God, give us some fire, and we'll burn up these miserable Samaritans.")

No. Don't sing them that song. And yet, Jesus looked at these miserable disciples, struggling and falling and failing, and said, "Rejoice because your names are written in heaven." Suppose Jesus came to you right now and said, "Rejoice, your name is written in heaven." Wouldn't that be good? Wouldn't you want to hug Him? Wouldn't you like to join the thief on the cross, have his assurance, and share the advantage of living a perfect life in Christ?

When the disciples came into that upper room, and Jesus went around and washed their feet, they began to cave in. (He wept over the feet of Judas, but Judas walked away. Even though Jesus promised He'd never leave nor forsake us, it's still possible for us to leave Him and forsake Him.) Then as He finished washing the feet of the rest of those babbling, bumbling disciples, He said, "Now, you are clean." *Now* they are clean? Before the night is over, one will be cursing and swearing and saying he never knew Him—the rest will be running the hundred-yard dash away from Jesus and the mob!

But, not for long! John is back, pressing as close as he can to Jesus in the hall of Caiaphas. And Peter is back, pressing as close as he can out there by the fire. And later, after Peter denies Jesus and finds out Jesus knows him better than he knows himself, he's on his face in the garden hugging the ground where Jesus was praying just a little while before, wishing he could die. Why? Because he had disappointed his best friend! What do you see in these disciples? People who continued to press close to their Master in a saving relationship, *in spite of their failures.* And even before the denial they have the assurance of forgiveness. *Before* the denial, they have this assurance!

Friend, you can take courage, today, in this saving relationship. Jesus promised never to leave you, nor forsake you. Now it's your turn to make the decision, "I will never leave nor forsake Him!"

And if you do, you're just as ready for Jesus to come right now, as you'll ever be.

Chapter Three

Why the DELAY?

When gunpowder was first invented, the "last-day" people said, "This is it." When the first steam engine went across the United States, the "last-day" people said, "This is it." When the atom bomb went off, they were sure this was it. The common market hit Europe, "This is it!" The stock market plunged, "This is it!" The Pope appeared on the cover of Time, "This is it!" "Seconds to midnight" they said—and yet it's been seconds to midnight for a long time now!

After a while, some of us became fed up with the "wolf! wolf!" syndrome. How often can you say, "This is it"? Is Christ's coming really near? Is the end of the world that close? Maybe it's time we thought a little more about "delay" and "waiting."

Let's turn to Hebrews for a closer look at this topic. "So do not throw away your confidence; it will be richly rewarded. You need to persevere so that when you have done the will of God, you will receive what he has promised. For in just a very little while, 'He who is coming will come and will not delay. But my righteous one will live by faith. And if he shrinks back, I will not be pleased with him.' But we are not of those who shrink back and are destroyed, but of those who believe and are saved. (Hebrews 10:35-39.) So, in just a "very little while" Jesus will come again—but even a little while requires some waiting!

The Bible uses, more than once, the language of waiting. We are all in the waiting room. But most of us have a hard time waiting, don't we? It's a little easier when you know exactly how long you're going to wait, even if it's two hours. If you know that at the end of that two hours "this is it", that helps. But if you don't know anything at all about the time, if the day and hour escape you, then waiting can be very painful. And people have found this to be true again and again concerning the great promise of Jesus' coming.

Why Study "Last Day Events"?

We said earlier that we don't have to worry about getting ready — that we're already ready if we really know God. If Jesus is my personal friend, and I spend quality time alone with Him daily, and I place my trust in Him—then I have nothing to fear!

We also saw that many people are uncertain because of behavior-centered theology which decides how ready they are on the basis of how well they're doing—and anyone knows (if we're really honest), that we can never do good enough. And so we discovered, it's not so much what you do, as who you know. John 17:3 says this is what life eternal is all about, "that they may know you, the only true God, and Jesus Christ, whom you have sent." Relationship theology produces certainty, because everyone can accept the option of knowing God.

But wait a minute. If we don't have to worry about getting on "the last trolley out" because we have an abiding relationship with Christ, then why consider last day events at all?

There are several good reasons that are legitimate and Bible-centered. John 13:19, for instance. Here Jesus gave the disciples a reason for taking courage from the things He told them ahead of time. "I am telling you now before it happens, so that when it does happen you will believe that I am He." This is a good reason to keep an open mind toward the book of Revelation. Some of us have become rather disenchanted with Revelation—not because of the book itself, but because of what people have done with it. Everybody and his uncle is taking a turn at Revelation these days. There are books galore. And everyone seems to have a different view as to what's going to happen next. I suppose it might be a nice ego trip to know exactly what events are going to take place tomorrow, and exactly what date the Lord is going to return. But is that really God's purpose for our study?

This John 13 reason is a good reason. If we're open to the book of Revelation, then when these things happen we can see God working, and know that He was credible all along. I don't have to get involved in trying to tell you *when* the events are going to happen in the future. But I *can* get involved in saying, "look what happened yesterday, and what's happening right now, and how these events fulfill what Jesus foretold." The excitement of knowing that we're really on track and that Jesus understood these things long ago, can be real excitement and real adventure. And isn't that a good reason for studying last day events and the coming crises?

Another Reason for Study

Then there's a sort of lesser reason (maybe even a raunchy reason). It's the "heaven to win and hell to shun" reason. The exceeding rewards for right doing, the enjoyment of heaven, the society of the angels, the communion and love of God and of His Son, the elevation and extension of all our powers throughout eternal ages—are these not mighty incentives and encouragements to urge us to give our heart's loving service to our creator and redeemer? And on the other hand, the judgments of God pronounced against sin, the inevitable retribution, the degradation of our character, and the final destruction are clearly presented in God's word to warn us against serving Satan.

Obviously no one is going to get scared into the kingdom of heaven. (What pleasure would it bring God to have people shaking in their boots as they pass through the gates of pearl?) But apparently it's possible to use the springboard of the "heaven to win and hell to shun" motive to dive into the deep blue pool of God's love. It's encouraging that God will take us any way He can get us—and then improve our motives! So, even though no one is going to get scared into the kingdom of heaven, perhaps some of us will get scared into seeking God, and then He can give us better motives as we discover His deep, unchanging love.

Two Ways of Watching

Now there's a negative way of watching for His appearing and there's a positive way of watching for His appearing. Let's read one more passage that gives us a warning on the negative side. Matthew 24:42,44,48-50. "Therefore keep watch, because you do not know on what day your Lord will come." Jesus didn't even know. He said so in this chapter. "So you also must be ready, because the Son of Man will come at an hour when you do not expect him...But suppose that servant is wicked and says to himself, 'My master is staying away a long time,' and he then begins to beat his fellow servants and to eat and drink with drunkards. The master of that servant will come on a day when he does not expect him and at an hour he is not aware of."

Apparently what Jesus is saying here is that some people are only concerned with how soon it's going to be so they can get ready at the last minute. This kind of person's life would totally change if they knew Jesus was coming by the end of this year. Or would it?

Sometimes I ask myself what difference it would make in my daily life if I knew that Jesus was coming back and this world was going to end by December 31st. Would there be any sweeping changes in my lifestyle? On the other hand, if I knew He wasn't going to come back for ten-thousand years, and knew I was going to grow old and crawl into my redwood box, would I cram for my finals the last year or two, and in the meantime eat and drink with the drunken? Apparently this is what the Lord is getting at here. (And you don't have to 'eat and drink with the drunken' in order to eat and drink with the drunken! Aren't there other ways of getting "drunk" besides that?) Anything in the "go ahead and do-as-you-please because it's going to be a long time yet" category is dangerous. And apparently this is what Jesus is warning us about when He says, "Watch it!"

Now on the positive side: if your best friend is coming to town, and you hear evidence that it's about to take place, don't you look forward to greeting the one you love? This is a legitimate, happy, positive reason to carefully watch for Jesus' return. After all He's the One that wants to get married. He's the one who's looking for His bride in person. The last I heard, marriage is when two people get together in person—permanently! And Jesus is very interested in that. So, there can be positive reasons for clutching the good signs of the times to our heart and saying, "It's about here."

Hastening or Delaying

There's something else in chapter twenty-four (verse 36) that's worth noticing: "No one knows about that day or hour, not even the angels in heaven, nor the Son, but only the Father." Let's reverse the emphasis for a moment. If no one knows but the Father, then the Father *knows* the exact day and hour of Jesus' return. But what about those who have said, "Let us hasten His coming." How are we going to hasten His coming when the Father already knows the time?

I'd like to suggest that if the Father knows the day and the hour, then any hastening or delaying would only be from our perspective, not through His. This also suggests another point: in order to hasten or delay anything, you have to have a particular point to hasten or to delay from. To even talk that language you have to have a fixed point in time. If I say I'm coming to your house for dinner at six o'clock, but I show up at five o'clock, I've hastened my coming. (And you're probably not very happy about it!) But my hastening is based on the set hour of six o'clock. So even though we're told we had a chance to hasten Jesus's coming, God evidently knew we wouldn't! He still knows the day and the hour. So has He *really* delayed it (as far as His perspective is concerned), or does it just appear that way to us?

Revelation 11:18 tells us that the Infinite One still keeps an unerringly accurate account with all nations. While His mercy is tendered with calls to repentance, that account will remain open. But when the figures reach a certain amount, which God has fixed, the account is closed, and Divine patience ceases.

Speaking of Divine patience, don't you think that God has been more than patient with you and me? Hasn't God been patient though this world has gone wrong, continuing His appeals for repentance? Hasn't God been patient with a church that has failed to accept the privilege of "hastening His appearing?" Yes, I'm thankful for God's patience—but there comes a point when Divine patience ceases.

Like the stars in the vast circuit of their appointed paths, God's purposes know no haste and no delay. And the end of the world, the coming of Christ, the conclusion of this cosmic tragedy, is one of God's greatest purposes. (The only thing greater might be the cross—that public cross on a lonely hill.) But, the coming of Christ is one of His greatest purposes, and I believe that God's purposes know no haste and no delay. That's why I'm taking the position that as far as God is concerned the time is fixed, and He knows when it will be.

Finishing His Work

We can also be thankful that according to Romans 9:28, *God* is going to finish His work, not us. We've done a pretty sloppy job of it.

How do I know the Christian church hasn't finished God's work? How do I know we haven't hastened His coming? Because we're still sitting here! Oh, you can say, I'm glad it lasted long enough for me to be born. I think I'm glad it lasted long enough for me to be born too. But that argument could go on forever. If He "delayed" ten more years, think how many more people would be born. Regardless, we're here now, and we can be thankful He's made provision for something more than a few short years in a vale of tears.

As I said, we can rely on God's promise that He'll finish His work. So isn't it about time some of us stopped trying to do the "Lord's work" for Him? You've heard the expression, "she (or he) is doing the Lord's work." Come on—let's stop trying to do the *Lord's* work. (Yes, I guess we know what we mean when we say it, but perhaps we *have* overlapped into His department too many times. And maybe that's another reason why we're still here!)

And while we're at it, let's stop trying to do the *Lord's* work in our personal lives, too. Some of us have really gotten involved in this, and that's why we continue to fall and to fail. He's promised all kinds of gifts if we'll only come to Him and accept them. But so often, we waste all of our time and energy trying to do what only God can do. We need to remember that He's promised He will finish His work in the world *and* in our lives.

In the Fullness of Time

It is not God's will that Christ's return should be delayed so long and His people stuck in this world of sin and sorrow. But unbelief has separated us from God. In mercy, Jesus has delayed His coming, so that we who are sinners may have an opportunity to hear the warning and find shelter in Him.

So from our perspective, there *is* an apparent delay, and there was an apparent possibility of hastening it. But looking through God's eyes, He's known all along when it will all come to an end.

And when does it all end? Revelation 11:18 gives us a clue. It's not based on the clock, not based on the calendar, and not based on someone coming up with a prophetic delusion, predicting it's going to happen in a certain month next year. It's based upon something that only God knows, but that we can perceive if our eyes are open: "The nations were angry; and your wrath has come. The time has come for judging the dead, and for rewarding your servants the prophets and your saints and those who reverence your name, both small and great—and for destroying those who destroy the earth." Another translation is "destroy those who corrupt the earth." Here we have a picture of the final awesome conflict between nations and angry people.

Some Key Indicators

Recently I had a chance to listen to some of the talk in Europe about the common market. And I had opportunity to ask people, "How is it going?" Apparently everyone knows that it's a problem, but they feel it's unavoidable. Nations are in the common market because they can't help it. They are on the verge of economic collapse and they're staying in for survival reasons—but they're angry about it. And nations are angry everywhere! Indicators concerning the finish of this world's history continue to multiply. God has an unerring account with the nations. And when the figures reach a certain point that God has fixed, that will be it.

" But," someone says, "Jesus won't come until the character of Christ is perfectly reproduced in His people." And we look across the aisle and think, "That will be a long time!"

Then someone else says, "Christ won't come until the Gospel goes to all the world." And the statisticians get out their calculators and begin to realize that people are being born faster than the Gospel is being preached by all the Christian faiths combined.

But we forget that when God steps in to finish His work, He has resources we've never even dreamed of. Remember, in the days of Nebuchadnezzar, on the plains of Dura, a golden image was erected—and overnight the entire then-known world found out about the God of Shadrach, Meshach and Abednego. All God needs today are a few Shadrachs, Meshachs, and Abednegos, and the whole world could easily know of Him overnight—especially in today's modern media world of instant communication. When God takes the wheel in His hands, we'll probably be surprised by the simple, effective means He uses to accomplish His purpose.

So, there is a point past which God waits no longer. The world will come to a time of corruption and self-destruction. Apparently there will be a global catastrophe of some sort. It may be nuclear war, or economic collapse, or a world-wide natural disaster. (It could be something else, but these three continue to rear their ugly heads.) And then God steps in and says, "That's thirty for tonight." Should we panic? Or should we do what the Bible says: "...lift up your heads, because your redemption is drawing near." (Luke 21:28.)

A Personal Illustration

In 1959 my brother and I went on a summer tour to study the dust heaps of the Middle East. Supposedly, it was a tour for pastors. It wasn't either—it was for archaeologists! I had a little bit of interest in archeology before I went. I had none when I got back.

On the way back home from the Middle East, we traveled across Europe. We planned to go up into Norway, and try to find our roots (Grandpa Nels home and where he was born). But we didn't properly plan ahead. So we ended up with just a few pennies left when we arrived in Frankfort, Germany. We still had a week or so with no resources except a few peanuts and some vitamin pills.

Well, we blew our last few pennies on German pastry in Frankfort and sat on the park bench that night while we gorged ourselves. Then one of us sat up and watched, while the other tried to sleep. We waited, and waited, and waited for dawn to come and our flight to Copenhagen. We didn't know what we were going to do. The next day when we got to Copenhagen, we found that we could travel by boat from Denmark, up along the coast of Sweden to Oslo, Norway, for twenty dollars each, round trip. (Those days are over!) Our plane tickets were fifty dollars, so we cashed in our tickets and had thirty dollars each to spare as we headed for Norway. In Oslo we were able to find a cheap hotel, and a motor scooter to ride through the night to where our ancestors came from. Finally we arrived back in Copenhagen.

But now we had all day to wait, and all the next night, and all the following day before our flight to Amsterdam, where we would catch our connection to New York. I was tired of waiting. I didn't want to wait! So, I told my brother, "I'm going to try for a cancellation from Copenhagen to Amsterdam, and then maybe I can get a cancellation from there to New York." He said, "You're crazy!" I said, "With the resources we have, all we can do is sit here and eat peanuts and vitamin pills. I'm heading for New York." So, I went to the desk of KLM and sure enough I got a cancellation to Amsterdam. I waved goodbye to my brother, and was soon in Amsterdam.

To my chagrin, the airport was packed with people waiting for cancellations to New York. Some of them hadn't bothered with reservations. There were tourists, including whole families, who had been there for three days and nights, fighting with each other as they sat on the floor with their baggage and waiting for cancellations. So, I surrendered. I said, "I might as well wait here as in Copenhagen." And I began the long wait, all night, listening to the people fight.

The next morning I thought, "Well, I'll go ahead and confirm my flight to New York. I went to the KLM desk and discovered that when I canceled my flight to Amsterdam, I had also canceled my flight to New York! It began to look like a long hard winter. I didn't know what to do. With my limited resources, I might die in that airport before I ever left it! As I sat there, worried and stressed to the max, I decided to get better acquainted with some important KLM official. I watched the desk until I figured out which of the VIP's I wanted. I went to him and poured out my heart—everything except tears, and they were on the verge. I told him my plight. He said he was very sorry, but I had made that choice, and there was absolutely nothing he could do.

The rest of the day, every time he went by, I smiled my biggest smile at him. It was a desperate smile. Then I continued to worry and fret. Late in the afternoon my brother came in. He said, "I thought you were in New York." I said, "I don't think I'll ever be in New York." As I told him my plight, he began to worry with me. Every time that VIP went by, I would smile the best smile I knew how.

Late that night between eleven and twelve o'clock they called our flight number. I rushed into line with my brother. I waited hoping against hope. Then I saw this V.I.P. coming up to the head of the line. He had in his hand the final word on five cancellations, and who would take their places. He read the first four names and I froze with fear. But when he got to the fifth name, it was mine! I grabbed my bag, I rushed to the plane, I got in my seat, I strapped myself in—and then I remembered my friend from the KLM desk. I hadn't even bothered to look at him, let alone to say thank you. I should still be there hugging him. I was plagued with guilt all the way across the Atlantic, but I was also relieved. I've thought about this experience many, many times in the years since then.

It All Depends On Who You Know

One of these days, the most fantastic flight you've ever heard about will leave this earth for that great city in the heavenly country. And there is only one thing that really counts: have I gotten acquainted with the V.I.P. in charge. What? You mean my arrival is not based on what I do? No, it all depends on who you know. And He's the One who stands at the door and knocks. If you know Him as your personal friend, you need have no concern about the flight.

And when we get there, God save us from rushing out to slide on the sea of glass, or trying out our new "hang-gliding" skills. Instead, let us rush to cast ourselves at the feet of Jesus, and thank Him forever for making it all possible.

Chapter Four

An End Time OVERVIEW

For some time now, people have been talking about the end of the world and of Jesus' coming. Many have focused on this as the grand finale in the whole plan of salvation. When you go to the downtown religious bookstores, the end of the world, The Late Great Planet Earth, and the second coming of Christ are top billing. The whole world is gathering around this momentous event.

In this chapter, I want to present an overview of 44 points, giving what we used to call in college a "survey course". We'll try to get an "airplane view," with a few words on each of these topics about the closing events of this world's history.

The Laodicean Church

(Revelation 3:14-21) As you know, the organized church that exists up until shortly before Jesus comes is called Laodicea. It is lukewarm and God's burden is that lukewarm people stop *being* lukewarm. Lukewarm just isn't going to cut it in preparing for the final crises.

The Final Crises

(Matthew 7:24-27) People who are serious about getting off dead-center are going to look carefully at building on the rock instead of building on the sand. This is an absolute must in preparation for the final crises.

Revival and Reformation

(Psalm 85:6; Isaiah 57:15) These terms sound alike, but are different in nature. Revival has to do with the inward life, the heart, the springs of action. It has to do with knowing God and spiritual things. Reformation has to do with outward change, with externals. Sometimes we confuse reformation as revival. Reformation without revival can lead to nothing but legalism. So-called revival without reformation can lead to nothing but emotionalism. The two of them go together and are very significant. Really getting to know Jesus as our friend will result in changes in our outward life.

The Early Rain

(James 5:7) The early rain is a Biblical term referring to the Holy Spirit's work on the day of Pentecost. The Spirit has been available ever since to bring the tremendous resources of heaven. He's one of our best friends. And He's the One who guides us "in the closet" as we kneel before God's word in personal communication with Him.

Satan's Delusions

(Matthew 24:23-26) It's been predicted that Satan will even deceive, if possible, the very elect. He's a master mind, and he's already figured out how to do it. One of his best methods will be to produce a false revival.

False Revival

(Matthew 7:21-23) Apparently this will take place before the genuine revival as an attempt to call attention away from the great and *real* revival. Miracles will be performed, devils will be cast out. People will be masquerading the gift of prophecy. Mighty works will be done. All of these wonders will be done by people who don't know

God. And that's the key to Matthew 7. They don't know God. They're being worked by another power.

The Secret Rapture and "Futurism"

(Matthew 24:26, 27) Read these words spoken by Christ himself, and you'll quickly realize that His return is no secret event. There's only one secret aspect about the second coming, and that's the *time*.

But the enemy has already planted a teaching designed to deceive the entire world. Ironically, he's gotten almost all of Christianity to accept an order of last day events that was born during the counter-reformation. As you know, in the early 1500's, Martin Luther shook the religious world to its very foundations. The counter-reformation was an attempt to try to recover from Luther's blows. During that time the prophetic events of the last days were re-interpreted by the Jesuits, and became the exact same scenario most Christians believe in today (futurism). In fact, you can buy books on this topic in the downtown bookstores right now.

So what difference does it make? Why not just wait and find out who's right? Because the enemy, a long time ago, called his ways and means committee and said, "This committee is here to decide how to deceive if possible the very elect. We need suggestions from the floor." So all the imps jumped up and began to make suggestions. But he made them all sit down again until one came up with the master deception—that they should teach people about God and faith and heaven and the second coming, *but* they should add just two words: "Time enough."

All kidding aside, there's a major glitch in the scenario of last events that's accepted by most Christians today. It's that after the secret rapture when the present saints are caught away, everyone else will have another chance. But watch out! The second chance theory has always been diabolical. We'll take a closer look at the difference between the Biblical order of events, and what grew out of the counter-reformation in later chapters.

Spiritism

(Revelation 16:14) There are a number of indications that spiritism, or the occult, is going to belt the world. It's very much in the thinking of those who've had their eyes open to the present situation. The spread of spiritism was predicted in Scripture long ago.

The Shaking Time

(Revelation 3:14-20) This is what happens to Laodicea at the end time. There's a big shake-up. Lukewarm people, which the majority of the last church is made of, are going to go one way or the other. This is one of the greatest signs of Jesus' coming that you can find today. Polarization is taking place everywhere, inside churches as well as outside the church. Those who are good become better through the power of God. Those who are bad become worse until the nursery rhyme is fulfilled: "When she was good, she was very very good. When she was bad she was horrid." There are only two classes of people when Jesus comes. Everyone goes one way or the other.

The Sealing

(Revelation 7) This takes place during the shaking. It has to do with the hundred and forty-four thousand who settle into truth and become solid, set, and unmovable. Through the grace of God, their commitment leads them to experience something they've never known before. This sealing also has a symbol involving God's day of worship. Revelation 7 points to the part of God's ten commandment law that's the seal. Two days of worship are going to emerge in the final events—one symbolic of salvation by faith, the other symbolic of salvation by works.

The Remnant Church

(Revelation 12:17;14:12) During the time of shaking, the remnant church will be revealed. This "last church" involves more than just church teachings or doctrine, however. The other aspect is the remnant experience. One could be a member of the doctrinally correct remnant church, but not be one of the remnant. Why? Because the remnant people not only have the true doctrine, but they have the true experience of knowing Jesus as well. This true remnant will be the last genuine people of God left on earth.

The Hundred Forty-Four Thousand

(Revelation 7) From God's perspective, the hundred forty-four thousand plus the great multitude that no one can number, are going to be front and center in the closing scenes. (Let's remember that Revelation 7 is mostly symbolic. So, why not the number as well?) This chapter is talking about a special experience by people who follow the lamb wherever He goes, and who are without fault before the throne of God. You may be one of them!

The Three Frogs

(Revelation 16:12-16) The three frogs come out of the mouth of the dragon, and out of the mouth of the beast and out of the mouth of the false prophet. They represent three powers that are going to get together during the closing scenes of this world's history: Spiritism, the papacy, and apostate protestantism (protestants who didn't go all the way in their protesting!) In the closing scenes, these three powers will to be closely united. Watch out! It's happening right now, and you're very much aware of it if you have your eyes open.

Global Crises

(Revelation 11:18) When a global crisis comes, the world will do some weird things that we'd never expect otherwise. What are the indicators of this global crisis? Right now, at least three things seem obvious: nuclear conflict, economic collapse, and natural disaster. What else the devil includes, we'll soon find out. But these three seem imminent. (Who'd have believed that sixteen thousand people could die overnight, as happened recently in India?) One thing is certain, there's presently a huge possibility of global crises which could trigger our world into doing some unusual things.

The Loud Cry

(Revelation 18:1-4) "The loud cry" is a term used to describe a particular message that causes the shake-up (when lukewarm people go either hot or cold). It's the message of Christ's righteousness instead of our own. And it's like a big cleaver—people will go one way or the other.

The Latter Rain

(James 5:7) Under the impact of the Loud Cry Message the Holy Spirit is poured out in tremendous power called the latter rain.

Witnessing Before Rulers

(Matthew 10:16-19) Don't worry about how to do this one. We're told that in that very hour, what we should say will be given to us.

The Image of the Beast

(Revelation 13:14,15) The image of the beast is a very real event that's pictured in Revelation 13, 14, & 15. It's when the United States, the leading power in the world at this time, will create a replica of the dark ages and lead the whole world back into allegiance to the Pope. Why would the U.S. do this? Because of global disaster. You see, when the devil has everything in ruins, either through nuclear or economic or natural disaster, people are going to finally get serious and begin beating their chests and saying, "We've got to do something!" And the only thing left to do is get on their faces and seek God. How? Go to the most popular religion, of course, and set up a replica of the dark ages, when people were forced to worship in a certain way. Why? In a desperate attempt to save the world from annihilation.

The Mark of the Beast

(Revelation 13:16,17) Simply put, this is forcing people to worship in a certain way on a certain day.

Religious Legislation

(Revelation 13:16,17) This is the attempt to pass laws forcing everyone to go to church. But whenever you see religious organizations forcing people to do something, it's always of the devil. God knows nothing of this kind of force—only the power of love! He has a sacred regard for our power of choice.

Leaving the Cities

(Matthew 24:15,16,20,21) As this coercion continues to build, there are indications that it will be time for God's people to leave the cities. (Some people kind of like this part. They're looking forward to leaving the cities!)

Early Time of Trouble

(Luke 21:25,26) Now, during this time when people are being forced, some Christians will not go along with it. This situation creates a time of trouble for God's people. Jesus made it clear that it isn't always going to be easy. In fact, Jesus said, "As they persecuted me, they will persecute you also." This time of trouble apparently is short, but it will be very real for those who are involved in the great work of the Gospel during the closing scenes.

Persecution

(Luke 21:12; 2 Timothy 3:12) There will even be persecution. This is predicted. But so also is the courage of the martyrs.

Sifting

(Mark 4:17; Matthew 13:21) This persecution will cause a sifting among God's professed people. Those who are not serious will be sifted out and will simply disappear. In this time of sifting the pure church will emerge without spot or wrinkle or any such thing.

Courage of Martyrs

(Matthew 10:28) During the sifting time the courage of the martyrs will be given. Those who become frightened at the prospects ahead don't need to be frightened, because the needed courage has been promised. Now, there's something interesting about this. The courage of the martyrs is *not* given *until it's needed!* Some of us are very familiar with this type of courage. It's a scary thing to think of getting up and talking to hundreds of people—scary *until* you get up, and suddenly the needed courage is given. If you've ever experienced this, you know what I mean. God doesn't supply it until it's needed. There's no point trying to anticipate times of deep need ahead, (even though there might be martyrs again) because we won't get the courage now, and we'll only panic out. When it happens, we'll have all the courage we need, even the courage of the martyrs.

Close of Probation

(Revelation 22:11,12) After this short time of trouble and all the world's events that are shaking the earth, we come to the close of probation. This is when God announces from heaven that it is done. "...he that is filthy, let him be filthy still; and he that is righteous, let him be righteous still..." (KJV) The polarization is finished. Everyone has gone one way or the other. And at the close of probation everything breaks loose.

Without an Intercessor

(Daniel 12:1) There's been a gross misunderstanding for some on this subject. It's called "living without an intercessor." Michael has stood up, and we're "on our own." People have gotten the impression that we're going to have to have enough juice left in the battery to take us through on our own power. But God doesn't operate on the battery principle at all. He uses the trolley car principle—always in touch with heaven through prayer and His word. We'll have the Holy Spirit and the angels double around us during the times ahead. Jesus is the one who forever lives to make intercession for us. (Hebrews 7:25)

The Four Winds Released

(Revelation 7:1-3) Up until now, the angels have been holding things back. (I wonder how many angels have their feet braced against the San Andreas fault!) Angels have been intervening, or we'd have been in a lot more trouble before now. When the close of probation takes place, the angels let go. If you think we've had trouble before, watch out! Now begins the GREAT time of trouble!

The Great Time of Trouble

(Daniel 12:1) "...trouble, such as never was..." By comparison, what we've seen up until this point is mere child's play. And as if all the economic catastrophes, natural disasters, and so forth were not enough, now come the seven last plagues.

Seven Last Plagues

(Revelation 16) Many people wonder about the seven last plagues. Have they already happened? Is the "noisome and grievous sore" cancer? No, if you read carefully, the plagues are much, much worse.

The Counterfeit Second Coming

(2 Corinthians 11:14) Why is there something dangerous about the popular scenario for last day events believed by most Christians? Because, if you study this subject carefully, you'll find this belief sets the stage for a counterfeit second-coming. The devil will masquerade as the returning Christ. He won't be able to do a very good job (not compared to the Bible description of the *real* event), but everywhere people are going to say, "Christ has come!" And if you don't go along with it, you'll be in *big* trouble! Watch for it. The new age believers

have already predicted it, have a time table on it, and know who's going to appear. But there will be those who won't go along with it—and they'll face capital punishment.

The Death Decree

(Revelation 13:15) This death sentence is passed on those who refuse to worship the image or receive the mark of the beast.

Leaving for the Mountains

(Isaiah 33:15-17) When this death decree is passed, it's time to leave even the small towns and head for the mountains or remote areas. So, the death decree is the Christian's signal to move out.

Time of Jacob's Trouble

(Jeremiah 30:3-7) Jacob's trouble is an interesting prediction.. We'll study this further when we explore Jacob's experience by the brook Jabbok (when he got in a fight with Jesus). Apparently, something similar is going to happen to God's people. Even though probation is closed, they'll experience some kind of desperate struggle.

The Battle of Armageddon

(Revelation 16:12-16) This battle comes under the sixth plague. Most Bible commentators believe this is a battle between the forces of good and evil—the last great showdown between Christ and Satan. It will encompass all the trouble and anxiety of a world gone wrong.

God's People Delivered

(Isaiah 25:9) Here we have the exciting time when God steps in. It's one of the most awesome experiences you can imagine. How thrilling it will be to be alive during that time.

The Special Resurrection

(Daniel 12:2) Did you know that there are three resurrections?

This is the special resurrection before Jesus comes. Two classes of people are going to be raised: First, those who pierced Jesus. He promised them they would see Him again, coming in the clouds of heaven. Second, those who have been faithful in the proclamation of last day truth.

The Amazing Second Coming of Christ

(1 Thessalonians 4:16) "For the Lord Himself will come down from heaven, with a loud command, with the voice of the archangel and with the trumpet call of God." Nothing silent or secret about this at all! It's the most world shaking event that's ever taken place, as Jesus comes again.

The Resurrection of the Righteous

(1 Thessalonians 4:16, 17) The righteous ones who are dead will suddenly wake up. Wouldn't you like to be in the cemetery on that day? "Hey," you say. "That's weird!" No, I don't think so at all. I'd love to be there beside my loved ones when the righteous dead are raised and are caught up in the clouds. And the Scripture says those who are alive and remain will be caught up to meet them in the air.

The Thousand Years

(Revelation 20) After the resurrection of the righteous, there begins the famous thousand years, when all the righteous are in heaven and all the wicked are dead on the earth. The earth will be a desolate, bottomless pit. And the devil and his angels will have three-hundred and sixty-five thousand days of cemetery to think about it. Satan is completely bound by a chain of circumstances—there will be no one to tempt any more, no one to hurt.

The Third Coming of Christ

(Revelation 21: 2,3) At the end of the thousand years, Christ will return to earth the third time for the grand finale.

The Resurrection of All the Wicked

(Revelation 20:5,6) What a terrible thing to come up in the wrong resurrection at the end of the thousand years!

The Last Great Confrontation

(Revelation 20:7,9) Everyone who has ever lived or died will now meet for the first and last time. Millions are on the inside of the city looking out, millions more on the outside looking in. And all of them are looking up!

Satan, Sin, and Sinners Are No More

(Revelation 20:9) Would you like to be alive and go through these events? Would you like to see them happen, be in the middle of the action, and not be frightened—but only anxious to be with Jesus, your best friend?

Yes, studying last day events can be exciting and meaningful. As we continue our study in more detail through the next few chapters, pray that Jesus somehow will be front and center. Then when all of these things take place, we will lift up our heads and rejoice, for our redemption draweth nigh.

Chapter Five

Revival & Reformation

What comes to your mind when you think of R & R? During military operations, R & R is good news. Those two simple initials stand for rest and relaxation!

Every Wednesday, our church women's ministry leaders meet. And each week we hear how the stress has gotten worse and worse and worse. It's unbelievable. I wonder how much longer it *can* get worse! I'm glad I'm not a mother. Then one evening we had a group of these leaders going around the circle trying to put in one word what their week was like. Among twenty different people, we had eighteen different synonyms for stress. I didn't know that there were so many, including the one I offered. Then I felt terribly guilty, because someone described their week as "blessed." And when someone else followed this with "grateful," I really felt ashamed.

Maybe one of these days we're going to have to "flee to the rocks and mountains" just so our souls can catch up with our bodies! But, would it really make any difference? Isn't it possible to let our souls catch up with our bodies right now, regardless of surroundings? You and I have just as much time as the railroad bum or the president of the United States. The last time I checked, they both had the same number of hours in the day—and so do we! What we do with it is our choice, because of our priorities.

Another R & R

As we talk about R & R in this chapter, we're talking about something that could probably include rest and relaxation. After all, they were both promised by the One who said, "Come unto me...and I will give you rest." *This* R & R is going to happen before Jesus comes, and it's going to take place whether you're involved in it or not. It's revival and reformation.

Defining the Terms

Now as we discuss revival and reformation, we need to define our terms. The word reformation really shows up only once in your King James Bible. It's talking about a change in the system from the days of old to the days of the apostles. It was the change in sacrifices and certain methods of worship. We're familiar with this if we compare the old system with the period since the cross.

But reformation has other synonyms. As we discovered earlier, reformation has to do with the outward forms, and is different than revival, which has more to do with the inward life. Revival signifies a renewal of spiritual life, a quickening of the powers of mind and heart, a resurrection from spiritual death. It has to do with the springs of life, the inward person. Reformation, on the other hand, signifies a reorganization. It's a change in ideas and theories, habits and practices. And so, reformation is more concerned with what you *do*—revival with what you *are*.

But, as we all know only too well, what you are is the biggest factor in what you do! Reformation will not bring forth the good fruit of righteousness, unless it is connected with revival of the spirit. Revival and reformation have their appointed work to do—but in order for them to work, they must blend together.

A Look at Revival

As we think of revival, let's examine Psalm 85:6. This verse gives us a prayer that wouldn't be bad for us to pray right now, individually, as we consider God's word. "Will you not revive us again, that your people may rejoice in you?"

Look toward heaven, if you're feeling colder than you used to. Look toward heaven, if you know of a backslider, or a hesitator, or a procrastinator. Look toward heaven with this prayer, for yourself and for others, "Will you not revive us again, O Lord, that your people may rejoice in you?"

Does the church *need* reviving? From our study thus far, we know that the organized church (the organic church) just before Jesus comes, is going to be known for its lukewarm attitude. Revelation 3 is clear on this point. And looking back in history, this is a church that once knew its first love. That's one of the complaints of the heavenly witness—that we have lost our first love. Why is that wrong?

Some say it's normal to lose your first love. Whether it's marriage, the church, or your Christian experience, they say, you can't expect that first fire, that first excitement, that first love to last forever. In fact, some think that perhaps it wouldn't be well for it to last forever. If your marriage continued exactly the same way it began, you'd soon have a short-circuit, and blow a fuse. C.S Lewis addresses this, and questions if anyone could last in a marriage if it continued that way.

Others have compared love to a welding torch. When you start the torch, it's a big orange flame which is worth nothing. You have to adjust it down to a steady blue flame in order for it to do the work.

And there are those who argue that these are good examples of the way we should look at our Christian life too. "Don't worry if you've lost the first excitement," they say. "It's only natural."

But, that's not the way Revelation 3 sounds. Revelation 3 says that people who've once known that excitement but have now lost it, make

God sick! Lukewarm makes Him want to throw up. He says, "I will spue thee out of my mouth." (KJV) So, God is very concerned about a lukewarm church. And one of the factors, in the final picture, is that this is going to change. Regardless of what you do about it, or what I do about it, it's going to change. There will be a stirring revival and reformation among God's genuine people before Jesus returns.

Revival is not a bad idea, when you think of normal, living people. We're not always the same, we change. If we were all statues in Westminster Abbey, we wouldn't complain about our rheumatism or arthritis. We wouldn't complain about the mood we're in. We'd all be simply dead. But, because we are alive, we understand a little bit about the seasons: Spring, Summer, Winter, and Autumn. Even the beautiful trees, with their delicate leaves, don't always look so lovely. Sometimes we forget that flowers don't always bloom. We long for the excitement of life at its full. So, today, let us look toward heaven with that prayer, "Will you not revive us, Oh Lord?"

The Enemy Within

There's another reason we should give careful thought to revival. It's that we have more to worry about from *within* the church than we do *outside* the church. The hindrances to strength and success are far greater from inside the church than from the world. We don't have the first reason for self-congratulations or self-exaltation. We should humble ourselves under the mighty hand of God, and He will appear to comfort and bless the true seekers. Instead of our glories and successes being heralded and hitting the headlines, perhaps we should go to our knees more often and admit that we're still here. People are still dying. Pain and separation and heartache and tears are still going on. So, we hear the call, "Will you not revive us, Oh Lord?"

Now, obviously the whole church will never be revived. There are the "hangers on" in Zion. There are those who go to church for other reasons than the best. Some are trapped because of family and employment. Some have selfish motives for belonging to the church. There will be those who'll drop out when they see signs of revival. There are those who'll move away. There are those who can't move away, and so begin to resist and to criticize and to dodge and to feint. (And they'll criticize even the way the disciples wash their hands or the way someone's ears hang on their head. Anything to dodge the real issue of our great need.)

But there will be some—one here and one there, a group here and a group there—who will respond. Those who are for real, who are doing serious business with God, will accept the plea of the Holy Spirit and revival will come. At the same time, before Jesus arrives, there's going to be a tremendous polarization. Everyone will either go one way or the other.

The Work of Reformation

In my long association with the church (growing up on the sawdust trail), I've become very familiar with reformation. I can give you all the buzz words. Here are some: church reform, dress reform, health reform, education reform, medical reform. Has anyone been around that long? We were told that we needed to change this and change that external thing. We needed to change our habits and our practices. We needed reformation.

If our primary preoccupation is with reform, whether it's the denomination, the institutions, the local church, or the family—if our primary preoccupation is with reformation, then sooner or later, something is going to blow! You can't sit on a keg of dynamite without the danger of it blowing up on you. Trying to hold yourself back by external restraints is just not going to cut it. And trying to change the church and bring on revival by emphasizing reformation, is just not going to do it. Israel got the same idea, a long time ago, that God's blessing was on those who obey. So they began to have big reforms, trying to get people to obey, so they could get God's blessing. But we understand, in the history of these people, that every reformation was followed by deeper apostasy. That's still happening in individual lives. If you rely upon "righteousness by resolution", changing habits and practices by force of will, every reformation will end in deeper apostasy until you finally get so discouraged you say, "Forget it !"

Revival that goes to the heart and spiritual life is our only hope for genuine reformation. The Bible speaks of it in Ephesians 4:23, "...to be made new in the attitude of your minds." It's also mentioned in Romans 12:2, "...be transformed by the renewing of your mind" (Mind refers to the inward parts—what we often call the heart.) We're talking about *spiritual* things when we talk about revivals.

Being Religious vs. Being Spiritual

Again, we're talking more about religious things when we talk about reformation—and there can be a *big difference* between simply being religious and being spiritual. It's the same thing with the law and the Gospel. The law deals with reformation, and it's certainly not wrong. But by itself, it doesn't bring about true reformation. It doesn't have the *power* to change our lives. It can only lead us to the Gospel, where we fall on our knees and say, "Will you not revive us, Oh Lord?"

Martin Luther understood this. As he got older he became worried and concerned. He said that before Jesus returned the world was going to be replenished with great darkness. (From his own study of prophecy, Luther didn't expect Jesus to return for at least three hundred years. He probably wasn't far off.) According to Luther, if we don't constantly *emphasize* the Gospel, being justified by faith and uplifting Jesus, then it will simply fade away. He knew that the heart of revival is Jesus, and that lonely cross on a public hill.

Which is More Important?

"Well then," some say, "which is more important —revival or reformation?" That's a loaded question. It's like asking which is more important, eating or growing? Love or marriage? Obviously, both are important! One is simply the *cause* of the other.

Now let's get our priorities straight. A revival of true Godliness among us is the greatest and most urgent of all our needs. To seek this should be our very first work. That's it. Number one. But when true revival happens, genuine reformation is the natural result.

But watch out! Reformation *without* revival simply leads to dead works. It's easy to make this mistake because reformation is easy to understand. It's more hands on. If there's something in my life that I'm supposed to change, and I'm strong-willed, I can do it.

On the other hand, when you talk about revival you're talking about something that's more mystical. And we have a very hard time getting our hands on that, until we learn the secret of the closet and our knees. It's easier to *do* something than to seek someone we can't see. People often like to be busy *doing* something. "Is there something I can do to be saved? Is there even more I can do? Bring it on." But revival—this mysterious thing of the heart, this regular appointment with Jesus every day—that seems too mystical! And yet, He promised us that He would be closer to us than when he walked with the disciples by the shores of the Sea of Galilee.

Reformation without revival leads to dead works, but revival without reformation leads to a dead faith! In fact, there's really no such thing as genuine revival without reformation. False revival is often based on trying to renew earlier *feelings*, trying to revive the excitement and the emotions of the first experience rather than getting to the heart of the matter—the mind, the understanding. With this approach, we could easily become victims of the popular TV stuff with the huge, swaying crowds, trying to work up emotions and ending up worse off than we were before we started.

And beware of a similar formula that's popular today. It goes like this: "Let's get rid of all these externals that have driven us up the wall, and just talk about faith, hope, love, forgiveness and acceptance." But that's not possible. True revival leads to a *higher* standard, not a lower one. Genuine revival, based on contemplation of Jesus and the cross, always leads to genuine reformation taking place in our lives.

Of Love and Sacrifice

How can we understand the great sacrifice of Christ and the intensity of the Father's love? Recently I came across something written by my son several years ago that offers a different perspective:

"Tears stained my pillow as I grieved for my handicapped child. Night accentuated the loneliness I felt, and in sorrow I cried to heaven at the injustice she suffered. 'Please God, how my heart aches for her. She's innocent and deserves so much better. Why must she hurt so?'

"It was then that the angel came. 'I've been sent to tell you about another child born with a handicap,' he said. 'But, for this child it was terminal. He lived only thirty-three years, and during that time nearly died a dozen times. His parents were separated before his birth and over the years his father watched him grow, from a distance, knowing that things would get much worse before they ever got better.

"'Right from the start, it seemed, this child was to have an uphill battle. He was born more or less outdoors, on a cold night with conditions that could hardly be considered sanitary. When he was only a few days old his mother had to flee with him to a foreign country to escape the wrath of a demonic king who wished the child dead.

"'As this babe became a boy, his parents' hearts ached for more than just his physical safety. Because of his handicap this boy didn't do a lot of things that the other children did, and he was often left out or laughed at. He attended a special school, and the kids in the neighborhood or the church would sometimes say hurtful things because of that. He was a good boy and they loved him dearly, but he had to be carefully kept, and this particularly concerned his mother, who often seemed to provide most of the specialized care alone.

"'Once, when he was still a boy, his parents thought they had lost him for good. But after three anxious days it looked like he'd be all right and they breathed easier again. However, even during those times when his life assumed a degree of normalcy, his mother's heart felt the steady prick of a sword, for his future was an uncertain one.

"'As the boy grew older he came to understand that because of his handicap he would never be able to marry or have a family of his own. This was especially hard because he was above all else a lover.

"'For a time the boy worked with his hands, but eventually he took up a completely different line of work. His parents watched him with mixed emotions. At first it appeared that he was going to make quite a mark in the world, but in less than three years his parents realized that his work would be cut short. He had heart trouble, you see. And it finally got the best of him. His life had always been an uphill battle, but when he climbed that last hill, it proved too much.

"'His parents were not together when he died, but they were both on hand to see it happen. One of the boy's friends tried to be of some support to his mother, but no one was there to wipe away the tears of his father. The father had been away for most of the boy's life. It had been indescribably difficult for him, and he tried to come to his son at the end, but the boy was in such bad shape, he was unaware of his father's presence at first. When his son died, they say the father's cries could be heard around the world. Perhaps that's just a figure of speech, but perhaps for those who have ears to hear, it is real!'

"Then the angel put a hand on my shoulder, 'Child,' he said, 'If it's true that misery loves company, then you have some of the best. I care—but *He* understands!'"

Long ago that Father and Son made a covenant to resolve our dilemma. And they're anxious, along with the Holy Spirit, to supply what we need to face the closing events of this world's history.

An Essential Ingredient

In conclusion, I'd like to remind you of something that's dominant in any great revival. There've been revivals without great preachers. There have been revivals without great organizations. But there's never been a revival without prayer. Study it in the Bible and in the history of the Christian church. I've been reading about some of the great revivals lately, and prayer was the central element. And they didn't begin with a mass prayer meeting either. They began with one individual, somewhere, who got a burden. Another one joined him, and then a small group. And they began to pray for revival. (Revival comes only in answer to prayer.)

What kind of prayer? Let me suggest a classic from the heart of a man who needed reviving and reforming.

"Have mercy on me, O God, according to your unfailing love; according to your great compassion blot out my transgressions. Wash away all my iniquity and cleanse me from my sin. For I know my transgressions, and my sin is always before me...Cleanse me with hyssop, and I will be clean; wash me, and I will be whiter than snow...Hide your face from my sins and blot out all my iniquity. Create in me a pure heart, O God, and renew a steadfast spirit within me...Do not cast me from your presence or take your Holy Spirit from me. Restore to me the joy of your salvation and grant me a willing spirit, to sustain me." (Psalms 51:1-12.)

Words from a king whose wrong actions would have made the headlines! But he cried for revival, and God answered his prayer—his soul was fulfilled. And verse 13 of this Psalm follows: "Then I will teach transgressors your ways, and sinners will turn back to you."

Remember, prayer and sharing are the grassroots of revival. And both are accessible to us in this twentieth century and the end time.

Chapter Six

Satan's DELUSIONS

There are a number of expressions that people use to try to describe what it would be like to be caught without any clothes on. "Caught with your hair down" for instance, or caught with other items down. I was trying to get up enough courage to write that second phrase when I discovered it, of all things, in Revelation! It's as biblical as your Bible. Revelation 16:15. "Behold, I come like a thief! Blessed is he who stays awake and keeps his clothes with him, so that he may not go naked and be shamefully exposed." That's an interesting way for God to appeal to us—to make sure we have our clothes on when He appears. And God has provided those clothes. Isn't that good news?

Now, let's take a look at this question of the devil and his angels. Is the devil interested in last day events? Scripture tells us that the devil is as a roaring lion going around seeking whom he may devour during these closing times. And he's done a lot of homework. It goes way back. We understand, according to Matthew 24, that he's going to try, if possible, to deceive even the very elect. "At that time if anyone says to you, 'Look, here is the Christ!' or, 'There he is!' do not believe it. For false Christs and false prophets will appear and perform great signs and miracles to deceive even the elect—if that were possible." (verses 23-24.)

So, before the great final revival impacts the earth (under the showers of the latter rain of the Holy Spirit and the loud cry message of Revelation18), there's going to be a false revival. It will come with all the trimmings—exorcism, and prophesying, and many wonderful miracles. (See Matthew 7.) But it will still be false.

Reviving an Ancient Error

Among the deceptions the enemy has planned is one that goes clear back to the early days of the Christian church—an idea that blossomed later during the counter-reformation. It has to do with the interpretation of prophecy. During the reformation, Martin Luther threw such a bombshell into the existing religious order that it was shaken to its very foundations. And so the Jesuits, during the counter-reformation, came up with some revised interpretations of prophecy to help take the heat off the Papacy. Among these new teachings were the "futurist" and "preterest" schools of thought. Preterism put forth the idea that the prophecies of Daniel and Revelation had already been fulfilled in the past, so there was no need to bother with what Luther had said in terms of the present and future. The Futurist proponents, on the other hand, took the position that most prophecies would be fulfilled sometime in the far distant future.

Surprisingly, these ideas from the counter-reformation form the basis for the "final event" sequence most Christians believe today!

The modern version goes like this: First, Jesus will come secretly and snatch away His saints. Then will follow a period of seven years, called the tribulation. (They get this by detaching the last week of the seventy week prophecy of Daniel 9, and moving it clear down to the end of time.) During this seven years of tribulation the seven seals, the seven trumpets, and the seven plagues will take place. If you're not ready to go when Christ comes and "steals away" His saints, you'll still have seven years (although bombarded with terrible troubles) to get the message, repent, and get with the program. At the end of this seven years, Christ will come back (visibly this time). Now the millenium, will begin *here on earth*. And throughout this thousand years, there'll be even more opportunities for people to accept.

Of course, an inherent part of the whole concept is the idea of another chance—a second opportunity to make your decision.

The Doctrine of the Secret Rapture

Now the "secret rapture" portion of this scenario didn't come from the Jesuits or the counter-reformation. It only popped up in the last century, the "discovery" of a few so-called Bible scholars. One, a man by the name of Darby, published the secret rapture theory. This was followed by a new translation of the Bible, known as the Scofield Bible, which popularized the secret rapture and the futurist's version of last day events.

Darby and Scofield apparently believed that verses 40 and 41 of Matthew 24 were addressing the method of Christ's coming. So, let's take a closer look at those verses. They're taken from the middle of a private discussion Jesus was having with His disciples. He has just compared our day to the days of Noah, and reminded them of how the flood came suddenly "and took them all away".

Now verse 40: "Two men will be in the field; one will be taken and the other left. Two women will be grinding with a handmill; one will be taken and the other left." Well, that sounds like the sort of thing that people say concerning the snatching away of one person while the other is left. But, what about the context of this passage? Jesus has just said (in verse 36), "No one knows about that day or hour, not even the angels in heaven." And he immediately follows the verses in question with, "Therefore keep watch, because you do not know on what day your Lord will come." (verse 42.) It's obvious from the context here that Jesus is talking about *time*, not method. It's the element of *surprise* that's the focus of His remarks.

(I suppose we could also see in "one person taken and the other left" the possibility that though many of us look alike on the *outside*, there may be something entirely different going on on the *inside!* That's certainly something worth considering.)

But, again, the issue here is the surprise factor—not the *method* of His coming. 1 Thessalonians 5:2 also brings up the idea of Jesus' coming as a thief. But check the context. Paul is talking about time not method. And in Revelation 3:3, John also uses the "thief in the night" analogy. But he, too, is referring to time (unexpectedly...an hour that you think not.)

Sometimes we simply forget to read the verse in context. Here's another example from 2 Peter 3:10. "...the day of the Lord will come as a thief in the night." (KJV) Does the *Lord* come as a thief in the night? No! The *day* of the Lord will come as a thief in the night. That's the point of all these verses. Scripture says that at Christ's return, the heavens will pass away with a *great noise*—hardly the approach of a sneaky night prowler, and certainly not secret!

A Matter of Glory

What could be the enemy's motive behind all this? We've already seen how he was trying to get the heat off the Papacy during the reformation. Could there be more?

Well, we know that the devil is a glory-hound. Have you ever been around a glory-hound? Ever been one yourself? (I guess we're all born self-centered enough to become one.) Isaiah 14 tells about how Lucifer wanted to be like the most high. He wanted God's glory and His power and His honor—but not His character. And this was the reason for his great fall. Lucifer, who is no longer Lucifer, aspired to be like God. (Sometimes we sing, "Be like Jesus, this my song"—only let's hope we have a different motive!)

So when the devil takes his Bible, and reads the message of the first angel in Revelation 14:6,7 ("Fear God and *give Him glory...*"), he gets a bad case of the fidgets. Then he reads Matthew 24:30, 31. ("At that time the sign of the Son of Man will appear in the sky, and all the nations of the earth will mourn. They will see the Son of Man coming on the clouds of the sky, with power and *great glory...*") If I were the devil, I'd chew my fingernails over that one! And how do you think he feels when he reads Matthew 25:31? "When the Son of Man comes *in His glory*, and all the angels with Him, He will sit on His throne in *heavenly glory*."

Infinite glory and honor belong to the One who created us in the first place, and keeps our hearts beating right now. And yet God is not an egotist. Calvary answers forever the question of whether God knows how to humble Himself. But He knows that it's healthy for human beings to admit where they came from and who keeps them going—and it's unhealthy for us to think we can be independent of our Maker.

Next time you doubt there's a God, look in the mirror and ask yourself what keeps you ticking. Your own power? No way! A lot of homage rightfully belongs to God, the author of life, and the devil hates that.

Behind the Deception

The devil also hates the truth of Revelation 1:7—that Jesus will come in the clouds and *every eye shall see Him.* Matthew 24:27 says, "For as lightning that comes from the east is visible even in the west, so will be the coming of the Son of Man." And 1 Thessalonians 4:16, "For the Lord Himself will come down from heaven, with a loud command, with the voice of the archangel, and with the trumpet call of God..." Yes, the devil hates Christ getting all that attention and honor. So he has tried to come up with this clever deception—the idea that Jesus will sneak in and sneak out.

The popular concept is that one day John wakes up and his wife is gone. (Why is it always the ladies that are taken?) He rings up his neighbor next door, "Jack, is my wife over there?" "No, my wife is missing too!" "Where'd they go?" "I don't know." It seems Christ came last night and they slipped off to heaven. Down at the morgue there are bodies missing because Jesus came last night and sneaked them away. Airplanes go careening through the sky and crash because pilot and co-pilot were both Christians, and went off to heaven. There are accidents on the freeways because cars are suddenly without drivers. Some of us think this scenario funny. But, this is what the rank and file in the Christian world believes today.

The Pending Invasion

C.S. Lewis offers an interesting slant on this issue in his book, *Mere Christianity.* First, he talks about the quiet imperceptible workings of God on earth, the Holy Spirit working on hearts silently, and the kingdom of God growing. Then he asks, "Why is God landing in this enemy-occupied world in disguise and starting a sort of secret society to undermine the devil? Why isn't He landing in force, invading it? Is it that He isn't strong enough? Well, Christians think He's going to land in force, we don't know when. But we can guess why He's delaying. He wants to give us a chance of joining His side freely. I don't suppose you and I would think much of a Frenchman who waited till the Allies were marching into Berlin and then announced he was on our side. God will invade. But I wonder whether people who ask God to interfere directly and openly in our world quite realize what it will be like when He does. When that happens, it's the end of the world. When the director marches on to the stage, the play is over. God is going to invade all right, but what is the good of saying you're on His side then, when you see the whole natural universe melt away like a dream, and something else, something that never entered your mind to conceive, comes crashing in—something so beautiful to some of us and so terrible to others that none of us will have any choice left. For this time, it will be God without disguise, something so overwhelming that it will strike either irresistible love, or irresistible horror to every creature. It will be too late then to choose your side. It's no good saying, you choose to lie down when it has become impossible to stand up. That won't be the time for choosing. It will be the time when we discover which side we really have chosen already. Now, we've got a chance to choose the right side. God is holding back to give us that chance. But it won't last forever. We must take it or leave it."

A Second Chance?

This brings up the third issue in futurism and the secret rapture that we've already touched on briefly. It's the teaching that there's time to repent *later*—after the secret rapture, after the time of His visible coming—there's still time to accept Christ during the Millennial reign on earth. You always have another chance.

This is a diabolical deception, because the Bible makes it clear that we do *not* have another chance after this life. It's Eastern religions, not the Bible, that speak of coming back in another form, where we'll have better opportunities to improve ourselves. The enemy has concocted all kinds of these "second chance" theories in hopes of fatally delaying our decision.

Now, after this tirade against the second chance idea, perhaps you'll find it strange that I'm grateful for second chances. But, I'm talking about in *this* life. Has God ever given you a second chance sometime along the way? Didn't He give Judas chance after chance? Didn't He give Peter a second chance? Didn't He give Jonah another chance? Yes! Yes! Yes! He even gave those wayward children of Israel hundreds and hundreds of years of more opportunities.

Maybe that's why the wise man said in Ecclesiastes 8:11, "When the sentence for a crime is not quickly carried out, the hearts of the people are filled with schemes to do wrong."

The Danger of Waiting

God is so kind and so gracious that you can wait and wait and wait. But C. S. Lewis is right. There will come a time when we'll regret that we've waited. We'll wait so long that our motives will have gotten confused—and we don't even know why we're interested now.

So the call comes, "teach us to number our days that we may apply our hearts unto wisdom". And Hebrews 9:28 reminds us that Christ was offered up to bear the sins of many—the sins of us all!

But only for those who accept, and who look for Him, shall He appear the second time "without sin unto salvation". Those who look for *Him*. Not those who look for relief from trouble, although that will come. Not those who look for surcease from heartache and pain and tears and sickness and death and grief and grieving, although that will come too. Not for those who are looking for deliverance from their ailments, or deliverance from the aches and pains and bumps and bruises of being born on the wrong planet, although that also will come. But for those who look *for Him!* There's a big difference. Where is your focus today, my friend? Are you looking for Him? *You* can be among those who look for Him, and for whom He has promised to appear—and soon!

A Personal Illustration

It seems like about a hundred years ago, I was a freshman at a college in southern California. It was during the first few weeks of school. My brother had been there two years before me, and he knew everybody. But I seemed to spend a lot of time sitting in my room homesick. So one day, I said, "I'm going home." I put a pack of Greek cards in my pocket, so I could memorize my Greek vocabulary on the way, and I started walking the three hundred miles home to Fresno. I got a short ride over to the base of El Cajon Pass. But it didn't look like I was going to get another ride all Friday. I saw a freight train crawling up the grade, and thought, "Oh, I can do like the railroad bums, and get on the freight train." Then I remembered all those gruesome stories I'd heard of people having their legs cut off while trying to hop a train. So I just kept on trying to get a ride. Ten rides and several hours later, after standing what seemed like forever in the Mojave Desert, I found myself walking down our block in the dark, almost home. As I looked in the window, my preacher father was studying. My mother was quietly reading. With a full heart, I watched for a minute, then pushed open the door and burst in with my usual greeting, "Let's eat!"

My father jumped up. He was so surprised. And he hugged me. Mother, just sat there. I looked at her and said, "Mom, aren't you surprised?" "No", she smiled. "I knew you were coming." I knew you were coming!? Just what is it with Mothers?

One of these days, down the vaulted skies, Jesus will come. And like my mother, there are going to be people who are not at all surprised, because they *know* He is coming. Why not be one of them?

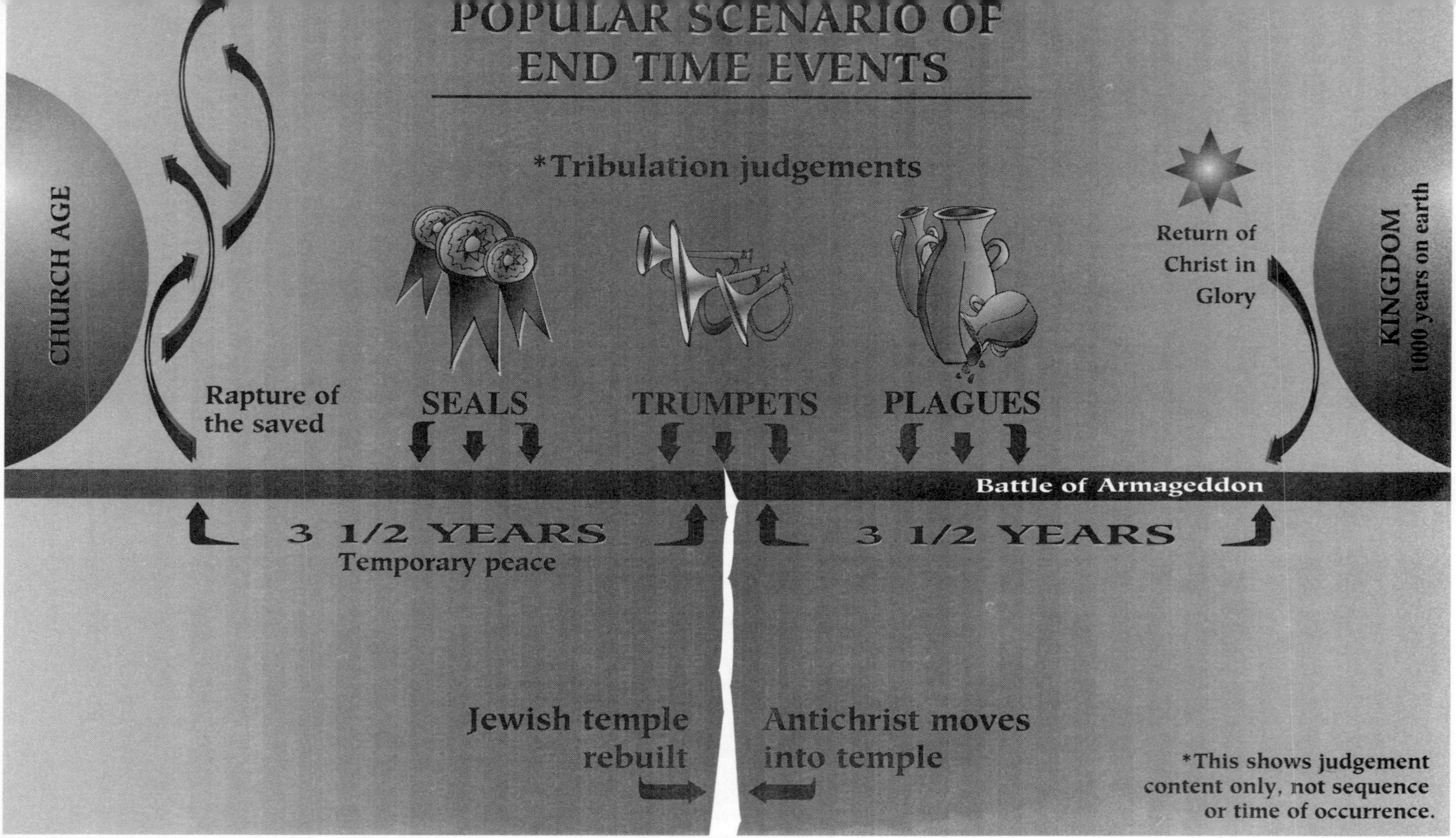

POPULAR SCENARIO OF END TIME EVENTS

CHURCH AGE

*Tribulation judgements

Rapture of the saved

SEALS

TRUMPETS

PLAGUES

Return of Christ in Glory

KINGDOM
1000 years on earth

Battle of Armageddon

3 1/2 YEARS
Temporary peace

3 1/2 YEARS

Jewish temple rebuilt

Antichrist moves into temple

*This shows judgement content only, not sequence or time of occurrence.

Chapter Seven

The 144,000

The one hundred, forty-four thousand. Who are they, and how can you become one of them? Almost since the day that John mentioned these chosen ones in Revelation, people have debated, argued, and had controversy over their identity. And as Christianity grows, the definition of the number continues to change. Some have even gotten a little light-hearted about it. In northern California there's an area some might describe as a Christian college ghetto, and late one night a sign appeared on the outskirts of town. It read: "College-town, California. Population: 144,000."

Now when you get down to serious business and begin studying, you'll find there are primarily two Scripture passages that deal with this topic. To begin with, let's consider Revelation 7. Here we have a description not only of the one hundred and forty-four thousand, but of a great multitude which no one can number. Verse one: "After this I saw four angels standing at the four corners of the earth, holding back the four winds of the earth to prevent any wind from blowing on the land or on the sea or on any tree. Then I saw another angel coming up from the east, having the seal of the living God. He called out in a loud voice to the four angels who had been given power to harm the land and the sea: 'Do not harm the land or the sea or the trees until we put a seal on the foreheads of the servants of our God.' Then I heard the number of those who were sealed: 144,00 from all the tribes of Israel." The tribes are listed and the story continues in verse nine. "After this I looked and there before me was a great multitude that no one could count, from every nation, tribe, people and language, standing before the throne and in front of the Lamb. They were wearing white robes and were holding palm branches in their hands. And they cried out in a loud voice: 'Salvation belongs to our God, who sits on the throne, and to the Lamb.'" Then comes more praise to God, followed by verse thirteen. "Then one of the elders asked me, 'These in white robes—who are they, and where did they come from?' I answered, 'Sir, you know.' And he said, 'These are they who have come out of the great tribulation; they have washed their robes and made them white in the blood of the Lamb. Therefore, 'they are before the throne of God and serve him day and night in his temple; and he who sits on the throne will spread his tent over them. Never again will they hunger; never again will they thirst. The sun will not beat upon them, nor any scorching heat. For the Lamb at the center of the throne will be their shepherd; he will lead them to springs of living water. And God will wipe away every tear from their eyes.'"

The Events and the People

This graphic description of the different groups has often intrigued students of Revelation. As we focus on these two groups (the one hundred and forty-four thousand and the great multitude that no one can number), we'll explore several aspects of last day events.

First, we'll review the big shake up—that polarization that takes place before Jesus comes. Second, the remnant church and what that phrase means in Revelation. Third, the identity and characteristics of the one hundred and forty-four thousand. Fourth, the great multitude no one can number. And finally, the "sealing" found in this passage.

The Shaking Time

The shaking time is basically that period when *three* groups of people become only *two* groups of people. Up until shortly before Jesus comes, there are still three groups: the hot, the lukewarm and the cold. However, when Jesus actually comes the second time, there are no longer three groups—only two. The lukewarm people will have disappeared! (Remember, this is one of the greatest signs that Jesus' coming is upon us, because this polarization has already been going on for some time. Are you aware of it?)

It's important to note that up until shortly before Jesus comes, the *majority* of people in the churches are lukewarm. Lukewarm people are people who look good on the outside (maybe even hot on the outside), but they're cold on the inside. And that's the combination for "lukewarm". Lukewarm people often look rather nice, but you can look good and still make God sick! According to Revelation 3, lukewarm behavior makes God nauseated—makes Him want to throw up. That's why it says, "I will spew thee out of my mouth."

But, because of the actions of the Holy Spirit, and the angels, and particularly the message "lifting up Jesus" shortly before He returns, lukewarm people will disappear. This mass polarization (everyone going either cold or hot) will be a major movement before the end of the world. When Jesus returns, He brings only two rewards: one for the "hot", and one for the "cold" (or the sheep and the goats, or the wheat and the tares, or the good and the bad, or the righteous and the wicked, or the wise and the foolish). Scripture describes these final groups in different ways—but there are always only two groups.

So, where do the lukewarm people go? They go either hot or cold. It's been going on for some years already, both within the church and outside of it. If we could look into each other's hearts, we could easily see the trend. Look into your own heart, right now. Are you finding the Bible more meaningful each day, or less? Are you praying more each day, or less? Are you finding more excitement in daily sharing the good news of the Gospel, or less? Are you getting colder and colder each day, or getting warmer and warmer? You can see the changes taking place in your own life. And this process will continue (both inside the church and out—and in the world at large) until the polarization is complete.

Anthropologists tell us that morals in San Francisco have slipped more in one year than in all fifty years before combined. And the Bay City is probably not alone. One of these days you'll be walking down the street and suddenly realize that the people around you are either "very, very good" or they're "horrid". Only the two extremes.

And what has caused this shake-up, or "shaking"? It's the result of the Holy Spirit withdrawing from those who aren't interested or serious about a relationship with Christ. (Angels withdraw from them, too, and double around those who *are* serious.) There's also the rise of a message some call "the loud cry"—a message emphasizing the righteousness of Christ instead of our own filthy rags. History reveals that whenever Jesus is lifted up, people go one way or the other. Wherever the Apostle Paul went (determined to know nothing save Jesus Christ and Him crucified), there was either a revival or a riot. No one stayed the same. And that's still true today.

The Remnant Experience

As this message (relying on Christ's righteousness instead of our own) continues to rise, people who are serious become more and more interested and involved. Not only do they find themselves absorbed in the good news of Jesus and all that He wants to do, but they become clothed with the righteousness of Christ in experience.

This is the remnant experience—knowing Jesus as my personal friend. It's not just church doctrines, or rules, or regulations. It's about making Jesus, not the church, the center of my focus. It's about being *spiritual* instead of just being religious. (Some people are very, very good at being religious, at going through the forms—but they don't know how to be *spiritual* because they're not really interested.)

The 144,000 Emerge

As the polarization process continues, the 144,000 begin to emerge. The 144,000 are genuine Christians who know last day (or remnant) truth, are overflowing with the remnant experience, and who remain after the rest of the professed Christians have left during the shaking. Clothed with the righteousness of Christ, these people are excited about the good news that all of the gospel includes, and with great power they begin to share it with other genuine Christians. Now the outpouring of the Holy Spirit, called the latter rain, upon the loud cry message (Revelation 18) takes place. Genuine Christians who know the Lord have been promised by Scripture to be led into all truth. Now they begin to understand Scriptural truths like they never have before, and begin to follow and join with these remnant people.

But when these "experiential remnant" people begin to come over and join up with these "doctrinal remnant" people, who also know the Lord, there's a group (we might call them the religious right) in the popular nominal Christian world that gets very nervous. Watch them, they're everywhere! They're inside the church and outside the church. There's even a rapidly growing political faction. They're the beginning of the "image" spoken of in Revelation 13 (which reminds us of the greatest atrocities in the history of the Christian church!) They're religious bigots who want power, but don't want Jesus. And these people, when they see the mighty power of God at work, get nervous and begin causing trouble.

As this "religious right" begins causing trouble, another group starts to get nervous. They're the people who don't know Jesus, but who know all about remnant dogma. They have no *real* foundation on which to stand, so they move out and join the nominal Christian world. They'll even tell the religious bigots how to give the remnant people more trouble.

In the end, as the groups become more and more polarized, all who have the remnant experience (know the Lord) will also understand the remnant doctrine (the commandments of God as well as the faith of Jesus—Revelation 14:12).

The Great Multitude

So far, we've explored the shaking, the remnant, and the 144,000. As the situation develops, where does "the great multitude that no man can number" fit in?

This group includes those who have joined with the 144,000, and who take the place (and more than take the place) of those who have left during the shaking. But the "great multitude" also includes all the believers in Christ from every age and every generation.

In the end, just as Jesus returns, there will be several types of people. First, there are those referred to as the 144,000, who are alive and translated to heaven (the holy). Second, there are the unnumbered people comprising the great multitude, who will also be taken to heaven (the righteous).

On the other side of the fence are the "religious only" people (the filthy). They're angry and frustrated with the whole thing until the very end. At Christ's return, they suddenly remember their Bible classes, and say, "Oh, it was true, after all!" And Scripture says they'll begin running from sea to sea and from coast to coast seeking the word of the Lord—but they can't find it, because they already made their choice long ago. And with them, of course, is the group that never accepted the salvation God provided at all (the unjust).

The Sealing Process

Now that we've looked at this polarization of groups, and its end result, let's focus for a few moments on the "sealing" mentioned in Revelation 7. It's obvious that the angels are holding the winds until these people are sealed in their foreheads (their thinking)—but how does that take place?

Study the sealing carefully, and you'll find it's an operation of the Holy Spirit. It begins at conversion, and continues to the close of each person's probation—whether at death, or the coming of Christ. The sealing is accomplished by the angels and by the Holy Spirit, and involves writing God's law in the heart—not just the actions!

Ezekiel talks about it. Jeremiah talks about it. There's going to come a time when God's law is written in the heart. If God's law is written in your heart, would your obedience be forced, or would it be natural? Would victory and overcoming be something you'd have to grit your teeth and work hard on, or would it come spontaneously as a gift from God? If God's law is in your heart, would it be hard to be good? No, it would be hard *not* to!

So, this sealing process involves the law of God. And there is a section of the law that contains God's seal (His name, His title, and the territory over which He rules). Which commandment contains this information, essential to any seal? The fourth—the one which describes the day of worship God established. (By the way, this worship day springs from creation, not from the Jews as some claim. There were no Jews around at creation!) This "Sabbath" was set up as a memorial to the birthday of the world. Every week, God gives us a chance to remember Him as our creator. And when you study further, you'll find the Sabbath is also a symbol of salvation by faith.

But there's another day of worship, a *false* day, that's a symbol of salvation by works. So the great issue just before Jesus comes is this: Am I going to accept the Gospel and salvation by faith (represented by the day of worship God established), or am I going to cling to salvation by my own works (and the worship day man has set up)?

Inherent in God's day of worship is the rest offered to those who are tired of trying to be good (Hebrews 4)—tired of trying to be overcomers in time for the final smoke, tired of trying to get their act together before the curtain comes down, tired of gritting their teeth and trying to change their lives. They discover what makes people on fire to share the Good News. They discover that all the means of salvation in the Gospel are supplied by God as gifts to every believer, and they begin to learn how to accept these gifts. The remnant church (comprised of remnant people, who know the Lord as well as how salvation fits in with remnant doctrine), becomes a church militant and on fire.

More About the 144,000

In addition to the passage in Revelation 7, there's another major reference in Scripture concerning the 144,000. The first few verses of Revelation 14 give us further insights about this group.

"Then I looked, and there before me was the Lamb, standing on Mount Zion, and with him 144,000 who had his name and his Father's name written on their foreheads." (We write our names on things that we own. Why? Because they belong to us. Here you have a group of people who belong to the Father.) "And I heard a sound from heaven like the roar of rushing waters and like a loud peal of thunder. The sound I heard was like that of harpists playing their harps. And they sang a new song before the throne and before the four living creatures and the elders. No one could learn the song except the 144,000 who had been redeemed from the earth. These are those who did not defile themselves with women, for they kept themselves pure. They follow the Lamb wherever he goes. They were purchased from among men and offered as first fruits to God and the Lamb. No lie was found in their mouths; they are blameless."

This is the scene, according to Revelation 14: Upon the crystal sea before the throne, on a sea of glass, mingled as it were with fire, are gathered the company that have gained the victory over the beast, and over his image, and over his mark, and over the number of his name (salvation by works). Having the harps of God, they stand with the Lamb upon Mount Zion—the 144,000 that were redeemed from among men. And there is heard the sound of many waters, and the sound of great thunders, and the voice of harpers harping. And they are singing a new song which no one can learn save the 144,000. It's the song of Moses and the Lamb, a song of deliverance. None but the 144,000 can learn that song, for it's the song based on their experience—an experience that no other company has ever had before. (Other *people* have, such as Enoch and Elijah, but no other *company* of people have.) These are the ones that follow the Lamb "wheresoever He goeth." Having been translated from the earth, from among the living, these people are counted as first fruits unto God and unto the Lamb. These are they that came out of great tribulation. They have passed through the times of trouble such as never were since there was a nation. They have endured the anguish of the time of Jacob's trouble. They have stood without an intercessor through the final outpouring of God's judgments (the seven last plagues).

But they have been delivered, for they have washed their robes and made them white in the blood of the Lamb. In their mouth is found no guile. (That's a Greek word meaning "fish bait." Fish bait is something that looks good on the outside, but is deadly on the inside. People who have no guile are the same inside and out.) They are without fault before God. Therefore they stand before the throne of God and serve Him day and night in His temple. And He that sits on the throne shall dwell among them. They have seen the earth wasted with famine and pestilence, and the sun having power to scorch man with great heat. And they themselves have endured suffering, and hunger, and thirst. But they shall hunger no more, neither thirst anymore. Neither shall the sun light on them nor any heat, for the Lamb in the midst of the throne shall feed them, and shall lead them to the living fountains of waters. And God shall wipe away all tears from their eyes.

In Summary

Let's make a list of the points we've discovered concerning the 144,000 thus far:

Number One: They are a special people who experience something *as a group* that no group has ever experienced before. They demonstrate victory, obedience, overcoming, and power.
Number Two: They have gotten the victory over the beast and his image and his mark—which are still in the future as you may know.
Number Three: They have, in some sense, stood without an intercessor after probation closes—which is also still in the future.
Number Four: They have passed through the great time of trouble.
Number Five: They have seen the seven last plagues.
Number Six: They have experienced the time of Jacob's trouble.
Number Seven: They are translated from among the living.
Number Eight: They are the first-fruits.

By the way, the 144,000 are also represented by the tribes of Israel. As you may remember, Israel (in New Testament applications), refers to those who are Christ's, and thus are Abraham's seed and heirs according to the promise. Revelation is not simply referring to literal Israel—it's talking about *spiritual* Israel.

Now, we've listed some of the earmarks of the 144,000. But there's something even more important. It's the *character* of these people.

First, they've received the seal of God. This means that they have settled into truth in a way that they cannot be moved. They have God's law *in their hearts* (including the Sabbath seal that's found right in the middle of His law.)

Second, they have pure doctrine. They are not "defiled by women." (No, this is not a chauvinist point. You know the women that are being talked about—Babylon the great, the mother of harlots, and her daughters. These women represent corrupt doctrine, fallen churches, and protestants gone bad.) God's people will have the remnant doctrine spoken of in Revelation. They have abandoned the corrupt and defiling doctrine of fallen churches, which Revelation symbolizes by corrupt women. And they are following a system of pure doctrine, or a pure church.

Third, they have complete victory. What does that mean? They are without guile, they are faultless. There's a word in the Bible that refers to anybody who has ever accepted Jesus, from the moment they first came. It's "blameless." The day the thief on the cross accepted Jesus, he was blameless. This occurs because of what we might call the "in Christ" motif. (How does that work? Put a leaf in your Bible, and from now on whatever happens to your Bible happens to the leaf. When we put ourselves in Christ, then whatever happens to Christ happens to us—or has already happened to us.) The devil comes along and says to the thief on the cross, "You're a sinner." "I know it," he replies. "And you deserve to die." "I know it," he says, "but Jesus is dying in my place." So when that same enemy comes to us, and we're in Christ, the conversation can go like this: "You're a sinner. You fall and you fail and you sin." "I know. I can't argue that." "And you deserve to die." "I already did." "When?" "At the cross, where I first saw the light and the burden of my heart rolled away." That's what it means to be blameless. Any Christian who got up this morning and said, "I accept your good news, Lord. I accept your grace." stands before God as though he never sinned. He's blameless! That's good news, isn't it?

But the Bible goes even further with the 144,000. They're not only "blameless"—they're "faultless." Why? Because they've learned through the message (and experiencing Christ's righteousness instead of their own) to be overcomers, to be victorious, and to be obedient.

"But wait", you say, "aren't we talking about only 144,000 people? That's not even a very big city these days!" Well, few of today's Bible scholars consider the number to be literal. If the entire chapter is symbolic, why not the number as well? Don't get hung-up on the exact number. Just remember that the 144,000 are a very real group of people with special characteristics and a special mission—and *you* could be one of them! It could be scary, or it could be good news. If you know about truth for these last days, and are serious about knowing Jesus, and are getting warmer and warmer in spiritual things, then you can be among the 144,000.

"But," you say, "I can't be faultless!" Neither can I! No one can, until they allow Jesus to move in. No, we're not without guile. No one is, until they accept the gifts that Jesus brings. Remember, we're not talking about people who *have to be* among the 144,000—we're talking about people who *will be* among the 144,000. And, there's all the difference in the world.

Where is your heart right now? The most important question you can ask today is, "Am I serious?" Ask yourself, "Am I for real? Am I *really* serious about this business of the Gospel and salvation? Is it my top priority every single day? Or as time passes, is it getting to be less and less interesting to me?" If you're truly serious, then you're among a most significant group of people—a group that the apostles and prophets would have given anything to be among. And you'll have the opportunity to see things that no one else has ever seen, as the closing events of this earth's history begin to occur.

What an exciting time to be alive!

Chapter Eight

Sealed for ETERNITY

There they were, right in the middle of Newsweek—the three frogs of Revelation 16! Tremendous evidence that this planet we call Earth is just about at the end of its present existence.

Let's get right into Revelation 16, and consider some of the last major events predicted to happen just before Jesus returns.

"Then I saw three evil spirits that looked like frogs; they came out of the mouth of the dragon, out of the mouth of the beast, and out of the mouth of the false prophet. They are spirits of demons performing miraculous signs, and they go out to the kings of the whole world, to gather them for the battle on the great day of God Almighty." (Revelation 16:13,14.)

Now, the action here takes place under the sixth plague, but the preparation for these unclean spirits, these confederated powers, begins sometime earlier. (Even as silent events are happening, such as decisions within your heart, world events continue to mount and move along at the same time.) It may sound like someone's dream or a fantastic myth, but these three unclean spirits have been clearly identified in prophecy. And the recent coverage in Newsweek gave me the courage to jump right into this chapter's topic.

The Three Unclean Spirits

So who are these three unclean spirits? The first comes out of the mouth of the dragon. Revelation 12 speaks of the dragon, that old serpent, also called the devil or Satan. But, the last I heard, the devil doesn't come to our door, knock, and say, "Good morning, I'm the devil, and I've come to give you trouble today." And He'd hardly appear at the United Nations, knock on their door and say, "Here I am. Weren't you expecting me?" No, he works through other forces. So, this first "frog" from "the mouth of the dragon" can be identified as the spirits of the devil, or what is commonly called "spiritualism".

The second frog comes out of the mouth of the beast. Back in Revelation 13 (the first half of that chapter), you'll find a lot of detail identifying Papal Rome as the beast. No, this isn't a recent figment of some subculture's imagination. The identification of Papal Rome as the beast goes clear back to the dark ages with Martin Luther and other scholars who carefully studied Bible prophecy.

The third frog comes out of the mouth of the false prophet. This unclean spirit has been identified in the last half of Revelation 13. It's Protestantism going bad—or going back from whence she came. And this is precisely what the prophecies have indicated that the United States, the world's dominant power, will do. (It's much easier to believe today than before the once powerful Soviet Union fell apart.) According to prophecy, the United States will go back on its original principles as protestant America, and will reach across to Rome. With the help of Spiritualism, America will be one of the three major powers that dominate events at the very end of time.

The Image to the Beast

Now as these three "superpowers" (Spiritualism, Romanism, and apostate Protestantism) begin to emerge (a trend clearly indicated in the national news magazine just the other day), something is formed which is known as the "image to the beast." In a sense, it's the Dark Ages revisited. Right wing evangelical protestants, who don't know they're fulfilling prophecy, will lead the U.S. in forming a replica of the Roman system during the Dark Ages—*religious dogma enforced by secular statutes and laws.*

Protestantism will stretch her hand across the gulf to grasp the hand of the Roman power. She then reaches over the abyss to clasp hands with spiritualism. Under the influence of this three-fold union, our country will give up every principle of its constitution as a protestant and republican government, and make provision for the spreading of falsehoods and delusions. This sets the stage for the marvelous workings of Satan. Through two great errors—the immortality of the soul, and Sunday sacredness—Satan will bring people under deception. While the former (immortality of the soul) lays the foundation for spiritualism, the latter creates a bond of sympathy with Rome (after all, worshiping on Sunday *came* from Rome).

Religion and Power

The image of the beast, then, represents a form of apostate Protestantism that will develop when protestant churches seek the aid of the civil government to enforce their religious dogmas.

These religious powers will so control the civil government that the "church" can actively employ the authority of the state to accomplish her ends. When the leading religious authorities of the United States (uniting upon such points of doctrine as are held by them in common), shall influence the government to enforce their decrees, and to sustain their institutions, then protestant America will have formed an image of the ancient Roman hierarchy.

And, as it was in the time of the Dark Ages, the infliction of civil penalties upon dissenters will inevitably result.

A Clever Conspiracy

Can it really happen? Here's what the news magazine had to say about events taking place right now: "In a prefab annex of the fellowship Bible Church, near the chicken coops...of Northwest Arkansas, a young man named Ralph Reed is preaching the gospel of politics. As director of Pat Robertson's Christian Coalition, Reed has come...to instruct evangelical Christians in the mysteries of winning elections." The article goes on to tell of an extensive strategy to take over the country (for religion) through mingling into politics at every level. It's the 700 Club and all that goes with it.

The article then describes the leader of this movement, "Behind the crinkly smile and avuncular manner is an angry, hardball player. Speaking to his own audiences, he can still use religion as a sword." And then the writer asks a question: "Can Catholics and Evangelicals use their common grounds to become political partners? Until a month ago, the closest Pat Robertson had come to the Roman Catholic Church was sharing his digs at Yale Law School with a graduate of the University of Notre Dame. That was in the 1950's, long before Robertson had his born-again conversion, became a Southern Baptist minister, and learned to pray in tongues. But now, Robertson's Christian Coalition...is openly courting conservative Catholics. At its September meeting in Washington D.C., the coalition bestowed its first 'Catholic Laymen of the Year' award on Representative Henry Hiey of Illinois. They also held a workshop on Catholic-evangelical cooperation and—holy heterodoxy!—closed their meetings with a Sunday Mass as well as a Protestant service."[1]

Fascinating! It seems prophecy is being fulfilled before our very eyes—and we're sitting in a ringside seat for the closing events of this world's history. Yet, even as these events are happening, there is something going on in your heart and mine. Moment by moment, we're either getting warmer and warmer concerning the things of God, or colder and colder.

[1] "God and the Grass Roots", *Newsweek*, November 8, 1993

Crisis as a Catalyst

Now, alongside these events are things that relate to global crises. We know that a major global crisis could put into action all the other strategies now in motion. Three possible global crises, obvious to anyone who has his eyes open, are *nuclear* (We thought this might be going away, but recently have gotten nervous about North Korean and Soviet stockpiles), *economic* (Who would argue that we're not headed for a worldwide economic crash? The prophets of doom, experts in this category, are everywhere!), and *natural disasters* (earthquakes, fires, floods, etc.) This last one would probably have occurred long ago if it wasn't for those angels holding back the four winds. And apparently, we've just seen the beginning. When major facets of global crises come into focus, people everywhere will panic, shouting, "Turn to God or we're all dead!" No wonder unheard of things—things people would scoff at today—will begin to happen, just as predicted. Even a cursory glance at the news media reveals clear indicators that, day by day, the stage is being set.

The "Sealing"

Now here's the spiritually exciting part. It's based on this "sealing" thing that takes place while the winds of strife are being held back. It's Biblical—but it's also kind of nebulous, kind of hard to get a handle on. So, let's take a closer look at the sealing, the sealing time, the sealing message, and the sealing truth found in Revelation 7.

What does the sealing mean? Some people believe a time will come when God will move in with some sort of electromagnetic machinery, and perform a type of brain surgery on us. We'll be made perfect overnight, and that will take care of everything.

Is that what "sealing" is all about? To help us understand the process that goes on in people's hearts and minds (while big political things are happening elsewhere), let's explore some synonyms for sealing. Webster's mentions words like secure...ratified...authenticated ...marked...and fixed.

Fixed? Now, that one rings a bell! My brother and I used to be darkroom photographers. (Did you ever get into that when you were a kid? Maybe some of you are into it professionally.) We went down and got a few supplies that didn't cost much. Then we rented a room from my mother (which was really a big closet), where we could get it good and dark. We put together our lights and our chemicals. It was fun to take some of Grandmother's old negatives, expose the sensitized paper, and watch her face appear through the developer. On our first try, we watched closely as Grandmother got darker and darker—and then the picture was all black! Suddenly, we realized that we'd forgotten to put the photo into the fixer, the chemical which (if you did it at the right time) would "fix" the photograph. Once "fixed", it would stay, would be secure, would be "sealed."

Let's think about that in terms of life and people and character. Evidently, one concept of sealing is "closed!" You can turn on the lights now. The picture has been fixed. It's finished. It's done.

Circumcision a Sign?

If you study the word "seal" and its Bible usage, you'll find that sealing begins at conversion. In one sense, we've *already* been sealed. Read 2 Corinthians 1:22, or Ephesians 1:13. Then there's Romans 4:11 which gives circumcision as the sign of having been sealed.

Circumcision? That's interesting. Apparently there are insights here we've missed. Isn't circumcision a health and hygiene matter? Yes, but this text makes it obvious there's a deeper spiritual meaning, too. Circumcision is symbolic of cutting off the whole resource that Abraham needed to produce a child. Abraham had to learn the lesson that although he *could* produce a son by his own resources, it would be the *wrong* son. He was then led to go through the experience of circumcision—a symbol that God used to try and show him (and followers after him), that the only true hope for spiritual things is total dependence upon God!

The Power of Choice

It's interesting to note that Jesus had been sealed by His Father (John 6:27)—His life set in cement, if you will. Didn't Christ have the power of choice? Yes, He did. Would God ever take away anyone's power of choice—even His own Son's? No. But there's a sense in which (as far as wavering from the plan), Jesus *could not* be moved. He was done, finished, sealed, set.

Now apparently Lucifer was not sealed before he fell. That makes you wonder about the angels and other unfallen beings. (Perhaps the angels and the unfallen worlds had their sealing when they saw Christ on the cross, and experienced the horror of what the enemy would do to his own Creator.) If Lucifer had been sealed before the creation, then he wouldn't—not that he couldn't, but he wouldn't—have caused all this mess that surrounds us.

A time will come, however, when Lucifer will be sealed in another way. You'll find it in Revelation 20, verse 3. An angel will come down and cast him into the bottomless pit—and set a seal on him! Now that's very interesting. This seal tells us that at the same time righteousness has been fully developed, evil has also fully developed. Complete polarization has taken place. Some people have become better and better (through God's goodness), and some people have become worse and worse (through Satan's badness). Now they are "fixed" for eternity. Not "once saved always saved", because the power of choice goes on forever. That's the way God made us from the beginning. But God's people will have His name written in their foreheads, and they will never move from their dependence on Him.

More About Sealing

Ezekiel 36 and Jeremiah 31 both tell us that God writes His law, or *engraves* His law, on people's hearts. In 2 Timothy 2:19, we're told that "the Lord knows those who are His". In fact, He knows them so well, He stamps His name in their foreheads. Then it says that those who belong to Him "...must turn away from wickedness."

As we come to the close of earth's history, Jesus looks down and sees His remnant people. They have the remnant doctrine and the remnant experience—but they're not sealed yet. They're called saints and they're called servants—but they're not sealed yet. Evidently their salvation is secure—but they're not sealed yet.

And so Jesus raises His hand to His Father and says, "My blood, Father. My blood for these people." Apparently the sealing doesn't have to do with our eternal destiny, but it does have something to do with God's glory and the happiness of the people sealed. (There's hardly a joy greater than the joy of conscious victory.) These people have already been brought to constant dependence on Jesus, and they've already been filled with the Spirit. The sealing doesn't cause that—it "fixes" what's already happened in them.

Some people try to seal themselves. Maybe this is why some move into the religious right. They delude themselves into thinking they can live without sinning, and they advertise it (one of their biggest sins). They try to perfect themselves—instead of clinging to God in absolute dependence. Those who overcome the world, the flesh and the devil (the three problems that give us all the trouble) will be the favored ones who shall receive the seal of the living God. Those whose hands are not clean, and whose hearts are not pure, will not have the seal of the living God. Those who are planning sin and acting sin will be passed by. The Bible standard for the 144,000 is extremely high!

Now is the time to prepare. God's seal will never be placed upon the forehead of an impure man or woman. It will never be placed upon the forehead of a world-loving man or woman. It will never be placed on the forehead of a man or woman with a false tongue or deceitful heart. The characters of those who receive the seal of the living God must be without spot or stain. They must fully reflect the image of Jesus.

Change is God's Work

Knowing these things, it would be easy to plunge into depression, and to become discouraged with this whole topic—except for one important point. This overcoming, this perfection of character, this not having one spot or stain, is all God's work, not mine! If it was *my* task, then I'd probably do something desperate like becoming a hermit, or a recluse, or joining the religious right. I might even turn into one of those fanatics who go around cramming their version of religion down other people's throats, publishing papers and stealing tithes, all in an effort to become perfect!

Something has missed us, flown right past us. The tremendous task of changing our character is all *God's* work. That's a big part of the Good News. The popular Christian world has latched on to the concept of justification, and has done a good job of focusing on it—but they're ignoring the rest of the story. Sanctification, the process of *changing* our lives, is God's work too! In fact, it's our only hope. It's impossible for us to accomplish it for ourselves. Fortunately, God has promised us that He will complete what He has begun in our lives, and will bring us through to the end.

"But, wait a minute," you say, " I don't like the looks of things ahead. Why can't I be one of those laid to rest before the troubles start—and get sealed that way?" I've heard a lot of people say that, even young people! Well, you know, that's not a bad scenario—*if* that's the Lord's will for your life. (I often think of my mother's words as we stood by my father's casket. A wave of fond memories came over her. "Sealed for eternity," she said, looking down into his peaceful face.)

And that's what will happen to you, if you're serious about God, and if you die before Jesus comes. But, that's also what will happen to you if you're *alive* when Jesus comes. As Jesus throws down His censor in heaven, He says, "He that is holy, let him be holy still." Done, finished, fixed, sealed. And you may be among them! But reaching this state is not something *we* must do—it's something that happens naturally if we're really serious about this whole thing.

The Bottom Line

Serious, how? *Serious in seeking God!* That's it, the beginning, the middle, and the end. Serious in making Him the top priority of your day—*every* day, not just on weekends!

Did you know Jesus wants to get married? He's wanted it for a long time. Yes, Jesus wants to get married, and He uses that kind of language throughout the Scriptures. When people in love write notes, they often put "S W A K" on the envelope. What does the "S" stand for? Sealed! During a wedding, why do we wait with breathless anticipation for that moment just after the prayer? Because there's something special about "sealing" the relationship with a kiss. It's a symbol of intimacy, oneness, commitment, and permanency.

Try this out for a definition of marriage: "It's when two people get together personally, and for keeps." In spite of what the world has done to this institution, that's what you *really* want, whatever your background. After all, that's what the ceremony is all about. It's for the purpose of "sealing" the relationship forever.

And apparently that's what God's sealing is all about, too. But, it's an enormous task—just too much for us to do for ourselves. That's why we must look to God to finish this sealing process, and must learn to depend wholly upon Him.

Chapter Nine

The LOUD CRY

We might call it the fourth angel's message (although the content most closely resembles the message of the second angel of Revelation 14). It goes like this: "And after these things, I saw another angel come down from heaven, having great power; and the earth was lightened with his glory. And he *cried mightily with a strong voice*, saying, 'Babylon the great is fallen, is fallen, and is become the habitation of devils, and the hold of every foul spirit, and a cage of every unclean and hateful bird. For all nations have drunk of the wine of the wrath of her fornication, and the kings of the earth have committed fornication with her, and the merchants of the earth are waxed rich through the abundance of her delicacies.' And I heard another voice from heaven, saying, 'Come out of her, my people, that ye be not partakers of her sins, and that ye receive not of her plagues.'" Revelation 18:1-4. (KJV)

This "loud cry" message comes after the shaking, when everyone goes one way or the other, and it will continue until the end of human probation. What is this message all about? Well, as we've discussed, the focus of the three angels of Revelation 14 is "Christ's righteousness instead of our own." And if you look closely, you'll find that concept is at the heart of this "fourth angel's message", too. So, in all these messages, the central theme is salvation by faith.

If you study the loud cry message, and the latter rain of the Holy Spirit, you'll find that when it's given, no one who receives it will question what's happening. It's a time when the message of God goes like a wind-blown fire in dry grass—it's everywhere! The sick will be healed, perhaps even the dead raised. A fantastic manifestation of God's power will take place that will make even the day of Pentecost and early apostolic church look small by comparison. So, in considering the drama of last day events, this is a vital message to study.

The People of God

Let's take a look at the players in this drama. The people of God, just before the return of Christ, are a lot like the people of Israel just before their entrance into the Promised Land. There's also a striking similarity to the attitude of the children of Israel, just before the first coming of Christ. (Remember how the enemy sought every occasion to take control of the minds of God's people, so that they wouldn't discern important truths?) So, people at the end time can be compared to two groups: God's people on their journey from Egypt to Canaan, and God's people just prior to Christ's first advent.

Now, these comparisons are not necessarily complimentary! But there's one comforting truth. In spite of their failures and their mistakes and their misunderstandings, they were still the people of God! (And you can be one of God's people, too.)

Here's another startling comparison. It only takes a little study to realize that the Church of Rome and the religious people at the time of Christ's first advent had a whole lot in common. And, if God's people (before Christ's first advent), and those living at the end time (before

His second advent), and the Church of Rome all have something in common—wouldn't it be a good idea to seriously heed the warnings found in Revelation 18?

It's a grave mistake to assume that just because we have some prophetic and historical understanding about these three angels of Revelation 14, we're secure from last-day delusions. Understanding the three angels' messages (which will swell to loud cry proportions under this fourth angel) is not enough. We must also have a *personal experience* in the spiritual truths these messages are all about!

The Three Angels' Messages

So, what are the "three angels' messages" really about? I'd like to propose that they go much deeper than warning about the judgment and Babylon and the beast. And, they certainly involve much more than simply encouraging everyone to attend church.

The loud cry of the three angels reveals the righteousness of Christ, the sin-pardoning Redeemer. This is the "light which shall fill the whole earth." Over the years, this message has largely been lost sight of, but it's not a *lost* message. And when it begins again, it will rush forward in strength to its final fulfillment.

All power is given into Jesus' hands that He may dispense rich gifts to mankind, imparting the priceless gift of His own righteousness to helpless human agents. *This* is the message that God wants to be given to the world—the theme of the three angels, which is to be proclaimed with a loud voice, and attended with a tremendous outpouring of His Spirit. It's the righteousness of Christ, imparted to helpless human beings. And Christ's righteousness is not just the beginning of this message. It's the primary content, the very heart of the three angels' loud cry.

Christ's Righteousness

The message of Christ's righteousness is to sound from one end of the earth to the other to prepare the way of the Lord. If this is true, then no wonder the devil hates it.! You're probably aware that in the last few years the devil has really taken a swing at this message. He's tried to bring it into ill repute, so that people would simply forget about it and go on to "more important" things. In fact, in many places people are afraid to talk much anymore about "righteousness by faith", afraid they might rock the boat and shake people up.

At a ministers' meeting in the South not long ago, one young preacher stood up and said, "Why is it some of you keep talking about the same thing all the time—righteousness by faith? Why don't you go on to something else? Why don't you talk about something more important, like church growth?"

Now I didn't know whether this young man was speaking "tongue-in-cheek" or not—I certainly hope so! But the point is that the devil doesn't want the message of Christ's righteousness to be clearly revealed or understood, because he knows if we receive it fully, his power will be broken. (And exciting things, including church growth, will follow.) If that's the case, then we have a heavy responsibility *never* to lose sight of this message!

The Right Focus

If we're really interested in taking the three angels' message to the world (under the loud cry of the fourth angel), and if we really understand the contents correctly, then righteousness by faith will be the main thrust of our message—our focal point.

But, exactly *how* do we focus on it? Here's an example. "Fear God, and give glory to him for the hour of his judgment is come: and worship him..." (Revelation 14:7—the first angel's message, remember?) Let's look at it in the light of this "righteousness by faith" theme.

What does it mean to fear God? It doesn't mean to be afraid of Him, but to hold Him in awe. What does it mean to give glory to God? It means to accept salvation by faith (from Christ) instead of salvation by works (from ourselves).

The work of God lays the glory of mankind in the dust, and does for us something not in our power to do for ourselves. And what is it we can't do? We can't save ourselves! We can't save ourselves from our past sins, we can't save ourselves from our present sinning, and we can't save ourselves from the world of sin. We're stuck! Born on the wrong planet, we're all in trouble, and our only hope is in the Saviour. (All false systems of religion have one thing in common—the idea that man can do something to save himself. And our greatest danger today is thinking there's some way we can save ourselves!)

"...and worship him." What does it mean to worship Him? Well, that means we worship God, instead of ourselves. If we think there's some way we can save ourselves, and we take part of the glory for our actions, then we end up worshiping ourselves instead of worshiping God. It's a danger warned about in the time of the three angels and it swells to a loud cry with the message of the fourth.

"Oh, I know I can't save myself," you say. "That warning must be for someone else." But these can be just words. The *actions* of most church members scream out what they really believe. When the majority of church members don't take the time, day by day, to seek Jesus and His salvation, then they're really trying to save themselves—regardless of the words they speak! If we really believe in righteousness by faith, then we'll spend time coming to Jesus, worshiping and glorifying Him, and learning to trust Him. Only then are we safe from trying to save ourselves.

Daily Devotions

By the way, did you know *everyone* has a devotional life? Don't talk about those who have a devotional life and those who don't. Everyone has one. Some people are devoted to rock music. Their devotional life is the sound pouring in their ears. Some people are devoted to the stock market. They spend hours reading fine print that would bore the rest of us to death. Some people are devoted to their own appearance. Their devotional life revolves around the mirror and the mall. Some are devoted to sports. Their devotional time centers around the sports page or ESPN. And many are devoted to television. A flip of the switch, and hours just seem to melt away.

What an insult to the King of kings by the very people who claim to be His children! They find it hard to spend time thinking and talking and listening to Him. If we're really going to worship God, then we can't spend our lives worshiping ourselves or others.

And that's the common (but often overlooked) thread of the angels' messages in Revelation—the warning against self-worship, and the invitation to worship God. Babylon and the beast are condemned because of their organized system of self-worship. But it's possible even for professing Christians to drift into the very "false-god" trap we warn others against. And we do it by finding time for everybody and everything, except the God we claim to worship.

Babylon

With that in mind, let's take a closer look at the loud cry message and try to understand a little more of its meaning and importance.

As we noticed earlier, the message of the fourth angel of Revelation 18 is similar to the message of the second angel of Revelation 14, and it includes a warning against fallen Babylon. But Babylon was fallen to begin with, wasn't it? Remember the tower of Babel, from which Babylon got its beginnings? Another attempt of mankind to save themselves, it fell a long time ago. But in prophecy, Babylon represents a fallen religious system. Babylon, the great, the mother of harlots, is not anti-religious—it's religious to its very core! But it has a big problem. The problem of modern Babylon (and ancient Babylon as well) is represented by the term "fornication".

Fornication is the merging of two bodies that aren't supposed to merge. And within the religious system of Babylon, the two things that they're attempting to merge are the concepts of salvation by faith and salvation by works.

The Wrong Focus

Most professed Christians believe that in "living the Christian life" we must strive to do good, and when we've done all we can, Christ will come to our aid and help us do the rest. This confused idea of obedience (partly by our works and partly by His auxiliary power), forms the foundation for the life of many Christians today.

Have you ever told your children to be good? Have you ever had someone say to you, "Be good," and you answered, "I'll try." Sounds familiar, doesn't it? We think that we're supposed to do everything we can in our own power, and then (where we fall short), God will make up the difference.

Particularly in the "living the Christian life" arena, we find it easy to fall into this pattern of trying to *make* ourselves do what we know we should. We grit our teeth and try to force ourselves to be obedient. And this "subsidy" religion (subsidy sanctification), is actually a part of Babylon. It's been around for a long time, but it's still Babylon.

The loud cry comes when God's people discover (through seeking Jesus, learning to know Him better, and coming into deeper, closer fellowship with Him), that *He* is the One who produces *all* of the righteousness! We don't produce *any* of it! Therefore, *He* is the One who receives all the glory. *We* don't receive *any* of it.

The truth of the equation is that "God's power plus man's power equals...NO power", and that's the reason for many of the defeats in our Christian life! Even while teaching against organized Babylon in our efforts to warn the world about the crisis to come, we hold on to the fornication principle—the principle of Babylon.

Deadly Combination

The combination of religious and secular power is deadly. During the Dark Ages, the "beast" power wasn't just a religious power, and it wasn't just a political power. It combined the two (fornication).

Spiritual fornication is rising again in our country. Earlier we said that when leading churches unite on doctrines they hold in common, and influence the government to enforce their decrees and sustain their institutions, then Protestant America will have re-created the climate of ancient Rome, and dissenters will face severe civil penalties. The very act of enforcing *religious* duty through *secular* power (a false union) creates this "image to the beast".

Let's carry this concept a little further. What's another word for "secular" power? Human power. Therefore, the image to the beast involves enforcing religious duties through human power.

We can talk about the image to the beast, and the mark of the beast, and the number and name of the beast, and we can look at it solely in terms of prophetic and historical events. But there's something deeper involved here. Could it be that we don't have to join the beast (or Babylon), to be involved in trying to enforce religious duties through human power? It's true that in the end, those who are a part of Babylon and the beast are going to choose a particular day of worship as a symbol of their power. But, it's possible to attend church on God's day each week, and still be guilty of trying to use your own human power to enforce your religious beliefs. And that's fornication. That's Babylon. That's the image to the beast.

Symbol of Allegiance

In the end, God's day of worship (see the fourth commandment) becomes a vital symbol of our allegiance. Those who honor God will come to fully understand the blessing and full significance of Sabbath rest. Paul put it this way, "There remains, then, a Sabbath-rest for the people of God; for anyone who enters God's rest also rests from His own work, just as God did from His." Hebrews 4:9,10

Those who rest from their own attempts at forcing themselves to keep God's law for salvation have accepted of the righteousness of Christ. And His righteousness will be lived out in their lives more and more, through *His* power instead of their own. This is the message of the loud cry. This is the message of the three angels in reality.

In this context, national religious laws predicted in Bible prophecy become more than just laws about a particular day of worship. They become the symbol for churches and people who have rejected God's Sabbath rest, and who are relying on their own works. They're an attempt to force submission to the Babylon principle, to save ourselves instead of accepting the salvation provided by God.

But even among God's people, this understanding comes slowly.

It's hard to learn (and easy to forget) that Jesus is our only hope of salvation. Yes, we sing about it, we pray about it, and we preach about it. But we often fail to *live* it!

Zacharias, the father of John the Baptist, apparently found it hard to remember—even though he was a righteous man, and a priest, and was specifically chosen by God to train and educate the messenger of the Messiah.

The birth of a son to Zacharias, like the birth of the promised heir to Abraham (and the birth of the Savior to Mary), was designed to teach a great spiritual truth—a truth that we're slow to learn and ready to forget. It's that in our own power, we're incapable of doing any good thing; but if we're submissive and trust in Him, that which is impossible will be wrought by the power of God. It was only through faith that the child of promise was given. And it's only through faith that our spiritual life is begotten, and we're enabled to do the works of righteousness.

The Focus of Faith

Notice that there are two things that happen through faith. First, through faith, our spiritual life is begotten. But it doesn't stop there. It's also through faith (not through our own efforts), that we're enabled to *do the works* of righteousness.

Not only does any attempt to save ourselves fail of its object, but it actually interferes with the working of God for our salvation! The effort to earn salvation by our own works inevitably leads to piling up human exactions as a "barrier" against sin. When people see that they're failing to keep the law, they begin to devise rules and regulations of their own to *force* themselves to obey. And all of this turns their focus away from God to themselves.

While some think they're committing themselves to God, they are really relying on *self*-dependence. There are many conscientious souls that trust partly to God, and partly to themselves. Instead of looking to God to be kept by His power, they depend upon watchfulness against temptation (and the performance of certain religious duties) for acceptance with Him.

There are no victories in this kind of faith. Such persons toil to no purpose. Their souls are in continual bondage, and they will find no rest—until their burdens are laid at the feet of Jesus.

An Invitation to Rest

But don't despair! For those who find no rest in their struggle against sin and the devil, there's good news! It's found in Matthew 11:28. And, it's Jesus Himself who gives the invitation. "Come to Me...and *I* will give you rest."

The rest from the problem of Babylon, (the problem of trying to enforce religious duty through human power) is found in coming to Jesus and accepting His grace day by day. And that's all we can *ever* do toward our own salvation. Just come to Him. And then, *keep* coming to Him. That's the secret.

In the end time of the three angels' messages, God's people will finally understand where the real power is. They'll experience great struggles. But, after all of the darkness, and confusion, and perplexity, and anxiety, something will finally dawn on them. And when it does, they'll receive the victory, and will go forth with a loud cry to proclaim the full message of the righteousness of Christ. And that message will echo from one end of the earth to the other.

Some of us believe we're living on the verge of that breakthrough right now. God's people have gone through many struggles along the way, seeking a clear understanding of the message of justification by faith, and of pardon and forgiveness. But in many minds, the subject of *sanctification* by faith, and how to live the victorious Christian life, is still shrouded in mystery.

There may be more crises involved as we approach a full understanding of the message of Christ's righteousness (as lived out in our daily lives). Yet that understanding *will* come, and the loud cry *will* begin. And it will continue (and be completed) as the message of "Christ's Righteousness instead of our own" is proclaimed with a loud cry throughout all the earth.

Chapter Ten

The Latter RAIN

There's a song most of us have heard which talks about a coming rain. It goes like this:

"Showers of blessing
Showers of blessing we need,
Mercy drops round us are falling,
But for the showers we plead."[1]

The outpouring of the Holy Spirit has been compared to rain, and the rain that we want to consider in this chapter could be called the "latter rain." What does that mean? It means God's Spirit is being poured out for the last time, the final time, before Christ's return.

The Holy Spirit has been around for a long time! He shows up in Genesis 1:2, involved in the work of creation. He was present in Old Testament times, moving in the hearts of men to convict, to convert, to cleanse, and to commission them for service. You can read about His work turning Saul, Israel's newly anointed king, into "another man." (1 Samuel 10) He descended in the form of a dove at the time of Jesus' baptism. And He appeared in a special sense at Pentecost.

It would take a long time to list all the examples given in Scripture of the working of God's Spirit. But we've been promised that the

[1] Daniel W. Whittle

Holy Spirit will come with particular power at the very end time, just before the close of probation, to do His final work in the earth.

So when we talk about the latter rain, we're talking about another outpouring of the Spirit of God as experienced by God's people in all ages—only this time it's in greater power and scope, and it's the last to come before the end of time.

God at the Reins

The first thing we need to notice is that God Himself is going to take charge, as He did on that day of Pentecost. He's going to take the reins into His own hands, and we're going to be surprised at the simple means He'll use to bring about and perfect His work of righteousness.

What does God "taking the reins in His hands" mean? Well, it's kind of an old-fashioned expression. I used to go to town with my Aunt Lucy. Aunt Lucy had an old gray mare named Nell, and when we visited Grandma's house (next door to Aunt Lucy's), we'd ride to town in the carriage behind old Nell. Since I was only three years old, I wasn't about to take the reins into *my* hands! I was perfectly happy to leave the driving to Aunt Lucy!

Perhaps a more modern analogy would be to say that God is going to take the wheel. There's evidence that He'll take control of events in a special way to bring about the finishing of His own work. I'm looking forward to that happening, aren't you?

There are some insights we can gain about the latter rain by studying the former rain (on the day of Pentecost). If the latter rain is like the former, the message will be carried not so much by argument as by deep conviction from the Spirit of God. The arguments have already been presented. The seed has been sown, and now it will spring up and bear fruit. Truth is seen in its clearness, and honest children of God will sever whatever chains have held them. Nothing can now keep them from obedience to truth. Family connections are powerless to stay them now. No longer will the excuse be given, "I can't accept this because my husband (or wife or parents or children) aren't willing to accept it." When the Holy Spirit comes with power, all human considerations will be set aside, and hearts everywhere will respond to His invitation.

Pentecost Repeated

In the last chapter, we discussed the fact that the loud cry message is similar in many ways to the second angel's message (Revelation14). But the loud cry message will be distinct. In a sense, this fourth angel's message will seem to be brand new, even though it's part and parcel of the message already given—Christ and His righteousness.

Apparently, under the showers of the latter rain (as at the time of Pentecost), people will hear God's Word spoken in their native tongue. The events of the day of Pentecost will be repeated. Thousands will be given the power to speak forth God's wonderful truths. The stammering tongue will be loosened, and the timid will be made strong, to bear courageous testimony to truth.

If you're timid, welcome to the club! Some of us are so bashful that it hurts. I used to complain to my father about it, and he said, "Don't worry, son, we're all bashful when we're young. You'll get over it." Instead, it gets worse every year! But I can testify to the fact that when you get up and try to say something for Jesus, He takes over and gives you courage beyond your natural personality. That's good news, isn't it? Even the most timid and retiring may be among the voices for God that will swell the loud cry during the latter rain, and cause the message of Christ and His righteousness to spread like wildfire among the stubble.

Here's another insight based on the former rain. Supernatural manifestations of God's power will be revived. Miracles will be wrought, the sick will be healed, and signs and wonders will follow the believers everywhere. What an exciting time to be alive!

But here's an interesting fact to keep in mind regarding the work yet to be accomplished. In this last great work, few "great people" will be involved. It's a dangerous age for anyone with valuable talents which can be used for God's work. Satan is constantly laying temptations for such people, ever trying to fill them with pride and ambition. And when God is ready to use them, often as not they're too independent, too self-sufficient, and too proud of their own ability to submit to God's plans.

"...God chose the weak things of the world to shame the strong." (1 Corinthians 1:27). How often have those with great natural talents, abilities, and gifts turned to their own ways, while those who seemed least qualified are used by God in the greatest capacity?

Have you ever looked back through your school annuals and pondered how many apparently "great" people on campus later disappeared, while some of the least promising went on to accomplish wonderful things in service for God and others? It's a pattern hard to miss if you have your eyes open.

Do you consider yourself to be a great person? Watch out! Are you afraid God can never use you for anything important, because you have little to commend you as a worker for Him? Good news! If you give yourself to Him, He can use you to do a good work for Him.

Under the showers of the latter rain, the restraints of our human machinery will at times be swept away, and the Holy Spirit will speak through the living, human agent with convincing power. And as the living water flows through God's own channel, no one will notice if the sentences aren't well rounded, or if the grammar is flawed.

Other Factors

Here's something else you can expect. On the day of Pentecost, when the Holy Spirit was poured out on the early church, thousands were converted in a day. God's blessing was manifest in a remarkable way. And yet, there were some who were unable to appreciate what was taking place. (see Acts 2:13) They concluded that Peter and the other apostles were drunk! So it will be in the time of the latter rain. The Holy Spirit will be falling on hearts all around, and many will not even recognize it, much less appreciate it.

Another intriguing aspect of this time is that angels will probably show up to do the work we were given the privilege of doing, but neglected. We'll hear someone proclaiming God's message with great power and say, "Where's he from? Who's he?" And the only answer will be, "I don't know." Angels have shown up in human form on many occasions in the history of this world. We have evidence of it in Scripture. And it still happens on occasion, even today.

Some years ago, a pastor in Arizona requested a religious liberty defender to come to his assistance. The pastor was nervous because a big meeting was being held by civic and political leaders in Phoenix to discuss religious laws for the state. The proponents sponsored a dinner, and chose an eloquent, well-known lawyer to present their case for "blue laws" in Arizona. This local pastor and the religious liberty representative also attended. According to their reports, the lawyer was so eloquent, and presented his case with such apparent logic, that participants were convinced to follow his suggestions and to proceed in enacting and enforcing religious laws in Arizona.

The local pastor thought that he should attempt to counteract the lawyer's presentation, but when he stood up to speak, he was unable to say a word. His whole mouth felt like it was full of cotton. After a few moments, he gave up and sat down. The religious liberty representative decided it was up to him to save the day, so he stood up. But his mouth went dry, too, and he also was unable to speak! As they slumped in their seats, wondering what was happening, the door opened and in walked a man wearing a pin-striped business suit. Approaching the microphone, he said, "I'm a citizen, and I'd like to say a few words." In just a few moments, he made the lawyer's arguments look totally ridiculous. The meeting became deathly still. The lawyer attempted to refute his arguments, but was obviously bewildered, and eventually the whole meeting broke up in confusion. Of course, the two "defenders of liberty" tried to find the man in the business suit to thank him—but he had disappeared! Surprised?

We can expect God's intervention in the times ahead, for all along the way He has given us little samples of His power. But, beware! This light which will light up the earth will be called a "false light" by those who refuse to walk in its advancing glory! There will be wonderful manifestations of God's power, but they won't affect those who've not humbled themselves before the Lord, and opened their heart's door by confession and repentance. As God manifests His power, their blinded eyes will see only something dangerous, something to arouse their fears, and they'll brace themselves to resist it.

Christ Our Righteousness

The devil is doing everything possible to bring the message of "Christ our Righteousness" into ill repute, so people will think it's dangerous and will fight against it. There's clear Biblical evidence of the way he has worked against this message over the centuries. But if the loud cry is the message which receives the Holy Spirit with latter rain power—if the loud cry is the message that Christ (not our own works) is our only hope of salvation—then we ought to do everything we can to remain open to it and to understand this message correctly.

And remember, not only is correct *understanding* essential, but also a corresponding *experience* in the faith that we profess. If we don't find the time, day by day, to accept and experience the saving power of Jesus Christ, then we won't be prepared when the time comes for the final outpouring of His spirit.

Chapter Eleven

Latter Rain *PREPARATION*

How can we be ready to receive the latter rain? At first glance it might appear that preparation for the latter rain and preparation for the coming of Christ are one and the same. But the latter rain itself is a part of the preparation for Christ's coming. Those who come up to every point, stand every test, and overcome every temptation whatever the cost , have heeded the counsel of the "true witness" (see Revelation 3). They will receive the latter rain, and thus be fitted for translation. The latter rain of the Holy Spirit, then, is one of God's chosen methods for getting His people ready for heaven. And in order to receive this outpouring, there must be some preparation.

Let's review the "job description" of the Holy Spirit. The first work of the Holy Spirit is to convict the world of sin (see John 16), and the second work of the Holy Spirit is conversion (see John 3). No one can even *see* the kingdom of God, unless he is born again.

The third work of the Holy Spirit is cleansing the Christian's life (see Romans 8). Unfortunately, while many Christians have responded to the first and second works (conviction and conversion), few allow the Spirit to complete His third work of cleansing their lives. Only when we see the importance of an ongoing, daily relationship with Christ can the Spirit change us into His image. And, it's under this third work of the Holy Spirit that the often-quoted "fruits of the Spirit" are developed: love, joy, peace, long-suffering, etc. (see Galatians 5:22,23). Included in this work is the "filling of the Spirit." It's a gradual process, such as filling up a cup or a vessel. It doesn't happen instantly. It's a growth process that takes place over time.

The fourth work of the Holy Spirit is to commission for service. And once again, there's a process involved. A new Christian needs to begin at once to share as much as he knows of the grace of God. Sharing is necessary to growth. But as a Christian matures and the cleansing process continues, the time comes for a fuller manifestation of the Spirit in the life (often referred to as the "baptism of the Holy Spirit"). Under this work of baptism comes the gifts of the Spirit, with the fullest demonstration of these gifts occurring during the final outpouring of the Holy Spirit in latter rain power.

It's important to keep these different functions of the Holy Spirit's work in mind, so that we won't lose sight of one very important fact. The baptism and *gifts* of the Holy Spirit, under His fourth work, are always for service. *The gifts of the Spirit are never for cleansing.* There's no Biblical example of baptism of the Spirit being given for any purpose other than service. It's not given to make you holy or happy—it's given to make you useful!

But, undergoing the third work of the Holy Spirit, (growth and cleansing) is an essential step, since we won't be prepared to receive the latter rain without it. The Spirit's *third* work is the time for overcoming, and victory over sin.

Preparation

With this in mind, let's consider an oft-asked question in regard to the latter rain. Does the latter rain change our character or direction? No, that's the purpose of the earlier showers that have been falling since the time of Pentecost.

In a great measure, many have failed to receive the former rains and thus miss out on the benefits God has provided. They expect their deficiency will be supplied by the latter rain. They wait for the *richest* abundance of grace, intending to then open their hearts to receive it. This is a fatal mistake. Only those living up to the light they already have will receive greater light.

In order to receive the *latter* rain, we must already be receiving the *early* rain through our daily relationship with Jesus. And through this early rain comes the power to overcome and victory over sin. If God's people simply wait for the latter rain of the Holy Spirit to come upon them, assuming it will remove their wrongs and correct their errors; if they depend upon this final work to cleanse them from filthiness of flesh and spirit, and fit them to engage in the loud cry of the third angel, then they will be found wanting.

Many continue to neglect the needed preparation and look to the time of the latter rain to fit them to "stand in the day of the Lord" and live in His sight. In doing this, they face the approaching storm without a shelter! Only those who have withstood temptation (through the strength of the Mighty One) will be permitted to proclaim last day truth when it swells into the loud cry.

Behavior vs. Relationship

Now, what's your response to the ideas above? Well, it probably depends upon whether you're looking through behavioral glasses or relationship glasses! The behaviorist considers them and says, "Oh, yes. I must begin anew to try to be obedient, to try to overcome, to work hard on being righteous." The relationist says, "My only hope for the times ahead is to know and trust Jesus even more. What a challenge, what an invitation, to continue coming to Him day by day to receive the gift of His righteousness."

We *could* look at these closing issues and think, "I must." But what we should instead accept is, "He will." There's a big difference between those two, isn't there?

So, although victory and overcoming and obedience precede the latter rain, that doesn't mean that victory and overcoming and obedience are our work, any more than the latter rain is our work. Our work has always been (and will always be), coming to Christ, day by day, for ourselves. And as we continue to come, and to accept the gifts He has to offer under the early rain experience, He'll prepare us to receive the gift of the latter rain.

When it comes to our part, the bottom line is always our continuing relationship with God. But He has made Himself responsible for all the rest of it, so long as we continue to seek Him, and to depend upon His strength and righteousness instead of our own.

Victory in Him

Let's look at several passages of Scripture that beautifully describe the victorious experience. First, Hebrews 13:20, 21. "May the God of peace, who through the blood of the eternal covenant brought back from the dead our Lord Jesus, that great Shepherd...equip you with everything good for doing His will, and may He work in us what is pleasing to Him, through Jesus Christ..." Who's going to do the work? *He* is going to work, *in you.* And what will that produce? That which is pleasing to Him, in every good work, doing His will. The work will be complete, but it's *His* work—it's His department! All we can do is go to Him, day by day, to receive it.

Now let's go to 2 Corinthians 10:4, 5. "The weapons we fight with are not the weapons of the world. On the contrary, they have divine power..." Whose weapons are they? Not ours, but God's! The battle is won through the forces of heaven, not through our own efforts.

2 Chronicles 20 records a significant Old Testament battle. The enemy was coming in force. But King Jehoshaphat had it straight, for

when he heard about the enemy, he went to his knees in prayer instead of out to the fields for target practice. They sharpened their scrolls instead of their spears. And God rewarded them, not only with victory, but with a very encouraging message before it was even time for the battle. First, He said, "The battle is not yours, but Mine!"; and second, "You won't need to fight in this battle at all."

The stories of the Bible are more than just simple history lessons. They're given to teach spiritual truths. Today, when we hear of the enemy coming "as a roaring lion, seeking whom he may devour", we should personally apply the message of 2 Chronicles 20, We don't need to fight in this war, for the great controversy is not our battle, but God's. And He will bring about the victory in our behalf.

In Christ, God has provided a way to overcome every evil trait and resist every temptation, however strong. But some of us, feeling we lack faith, remain away from Christ. This solves nothing. Instead, in our helpless unworthiness, we must cast ourselves on the mercy of our compassionate Saviour. He healed the sick and cast out demons when He walked among men, and He's the same mighty Redeemer today. We must not look at ourselves, but to Christ. We must grasp His promise, "Whoever comes to me, I will never drive away." (John 6:37). Coming to Him, we must believe He accepts us, because He promised to. And we can never perish while we do this—never!

That's good news, isn't it? God has the power to finish the work He's begun in our lives, and to fully prepare us for His coming.

Positive Change

Which brings us to one final question: If the work of victory and overcoming must be accomplished *before* the latter rain, but the latter rain itself continues to prepare us in some way for the coming of Christ, what additional preparation does the latter rain accomplish?

Apparently there are some positive graces of the Spirit that are needed in our lives before we're fitted for translation—graces that go above and beyond merely overcoming sin.

Perhaps a short analogy might help. If you expect company, you probably start with the more negative kinds of preparing. You may scrub the kitchen floor, or clean the sink, or wash the sheets. This type of preparation involves removing any defilement from your home and your environment.

But there's more to getting ready for company than taking out the trash. You also want to make positive preparations. You may wish to bake a cake, or set the table with your best dishes, or bring in some fresh flowers from the garden.

All too often, when we talk of preparing for Christ's coming, we think in terms of cleaning up the negative aspects of our lives. But, as we prepare for the marriage supper of the Lamb, perhaps there's room for some positive changes (beyond the cleansing of sin).

And these final changes, these finishing touches that the Holy Spirit will add to willing hearts, will make us fully ready to meet Him.

Chapter Twelve

Mark of the BEAST

You can't get through a book on last day events without taking a look at the "mark of the beast." For starters, I'd like to go back to the pilgrim fathers and the way this country began. And then, we'll look at the way this country will end.

To set the stage, here's a great piece from author Chuck Swindoll: "I've got a love affair going with Thanksgiving. Hands down it's my favorite holiday of all. Here's why. First of all, it seems to blend together all we Americans hold precious and dear, without the sham and plastic mask of commercialism. Shopping centers jump from Halloween to Christmas. It's spooks to Santa. Pumpkins to presents. Orange and black to red and green. Except for grocery stores, merchants are silent on Thanksgiving all around. Second, it highlights the home and family. Thanksgiving is synonymous with stuff that can be found only at home. The warmth of a fireplace, early morning fussing around the kitchen. Kids and grandkids, long distance phone calls, family reunions, singing around the piano, holding hands and praying before that special meal. Friends dropping by, pumpkin pie, homemade rolls, and six-million calories. It's a time of quiet reflection upon the past and an annual reminder that God has again been ever so faithful. The solid and simple things of life are brought into clear focus, so much so that everything else fades into insignificance. Third, it drips with national nostalgia, for me, even more so than the Fourth of July. That holiday reminds us of a battle we won, giving us independence. This one takes us back to a simple slice of life, over three-hundred fifty years ago, when our forefathers and foremothers realized dependence on each other to survive. With Thanksgiving comes a surge of renewed patriotism, a quiet inner peace that whispers 'I'm proud to be an American.' Thanksgiving puts steel into our patriotic veins. It reminds us of our great heritage. It carries us back with numbing nostalgia to that first grip on life at Plymouth, where less than half a handful of people survived. It speaks in clear, crisp tones of forgotten terms, like integrity, bravery, respect, faith, vigilance, dignity, honor, freedom, discipline, sacrifice, Godliness. How could it ever change?"[1]

But the sad truth is that this country will change, and it's in the process now. Prophetic insight has told us that the United States of America would begin as a lamb, but end as a dragon. And the irony is that the only way we can make it through is to have the faith of our forefathers and foremothers who started this country.

An Intriguing Topic

When we get into the "mark of the beast," a time when people are forced to be religious because of world panic, it makes some of us a little nervous. If you've never explored this subject before, then perhaps you're in for some surprises. If, like me, you grew up on the sawdust trail, with prophecy three times a day (five on weekends!), then it's all too common. I can remember my evangelistic father and uncle putting out their notices in the newspapers and selling tickets to the "closed door lecture on The Mark of the Beast." People always came to that one. "What is this 666 and mark of the beast?" People have been interested in that for a long time.

[1]Swindoll, Charles R. Growing Strong in the Seasons of Life, Multnomah Press, 394-396.

I remember one night in Fresno, California, while my dad was holding meetings on this subject, a young man came for the first time. Afterwards, he got my father in a corner and tried to ask him some questions. Dad was trying to be careful and sensitive. He didn't want to say too much too soon. But, the young man stared him in the eyes and said, "You don't have to beat around the bush with me! Just tell me the truth." This was his introduction to an interest in the Bible—The Mark of the Beast! (Later this young man went on to college, and became a minister.)

So, let's jump right into it by turning to one of the most severe warnings in Scripture. Revelation 14:9 tells about a third angel (preceded by two others) with a special message. "A third angel followed them and said in a loud voice: 'If anyone worships the beast *and* his image (please notice the "ands"—if you worship one, you worship them all) *and* receives his mark on the forehead or on the hand, he, too, will drink of the wine of God's fury, which has been poured full strength into the cup of his wrath." (God's wrath is in the seven last plagues) "He will be tormented with burning sulfur in the presence of the holy angels and of the Lamb. And the smoke of their torment rises for ever and ever. There is no rest day or night for those who worship the beast and his image, or for anyone who receives the mark of his name."

Well, there it is. You have to admit this is pretty heavy-duty stuff! And it's led many to ask, "What is this mark of the beast anyway?"

Identifying the Beast

In order to get a handle on this, we first have to find out who the "beast" is. To do that, we go to the previous chapter, Revelation 13. There we have two parts—the first is about a beast that's a composite of beasts found in Daniel; the second is about a beast that begins as a lamb and ends like a dragon. Traditionally, Bible scholars have believed (for a long time now) that the first beast of Revelation 13 is Papal Rome, also known as the Catholic Church, and that the second beast is the United States of America.

Now, right here I get a little tender, a little sensitive. I get the same feeling that I used to have when I tried to be an evangelist (before I found out I wasn't one). I feel kind of guilty for talking about someone else's religion. You know, am I being too hard on the Catholics? Am I being critical? Am I being unkind? The truth is that today's Pope is a rather friendly sort, isn't he? I kind of like him. And Pat Robertson, the leader of the religious right that's rising rapidly in this country—how can you beat the smile on Pat Robertson's face? Maybe they don't know the parts they're playing in last day events. God certainly must be trying to reveal it to them, or He already has somewhere along the line.

But, we're talking about issues here, not personalities. And the more I read Newsweek and watch the media, the more I see closing events unfolding before my eyes—and the less apologetic I feel about getting into these events.

An Unholy Alliance

Now, as I said, the first half of Revelation 13 is about the Papacy. I'm not going to list the major reasons why this is very clear—plenty of others have covered that over the years (including Martin Luther). And it's not something that was dreamed up by someone in recent years. It's historically grounded in the Protestant reformation, with reformers of that day shouting from the roof tops that the Babylon of the Apocalypse was the Papacy. (And it's also clear, today, to anyone who carefully compares prophecy with historical records.)

So, what was the Papacy? It was a combination of religious and political power. Predictions in more than one place (in both Daniel and Revelation) claimed that the Papacy would rule for 1260 years.

And it did—from 538 to 1798 A.D. The prophetic time clock was right on target. During that time, religious people tried to make other people good through secular power, forcing people's consciences, and burning them if they wouldn't give in. Some today apologize for these actions. Others say, "Watch out! Rome never changes!"

But, the problem in the end is not *Rome* taking the initiative. The problem is Protestant America, gone apostate, taking the initiative. The religious right is going to lead us (during some kind of world panic) to reach across the gulf to Romanism. In the end, people will again be forced to be religious. Apparently, it's for the purpose of saving the world from annihilation—which means that in order for this incredible series of events to happen, there will have to be some kind of major global crises.

We've already discussed three fronts on which this might happen—nuclear, economic, and/or natural disaster. We also noticed that there are four angels holding back the winds, or all hell (literally) would have broken loose long before this. One of these days soon, everything is going to cave in. The whole world will be driven to its knees in panic. And prophecy points to one leading political power (even more clearly since Communism began to collapse) which "arose like a lamb"—the United States of America—that will lead the world in *forcing* people to turn to God. And how can they do that? In the most popular, acceptable way, of course—through the leadership of the world's greatest powers. Suddenly, we have the "image to the beast" spoken of in the last half of Revelation 13. Then things really begin to get heavy, including a world-wide boycott, and the death penalty for those who don't go along.

Turn with me to the heart of this prophecy in the last few verses of Revelation 13. The image to the beast has been formed. The United States (which began in the search for four basic freedoms, plus a state without a king, and a church without a Pope), will return to the very thing they fled from. Verse 16 begins, "He [the U.S.] also forced everyone, small and great, rich and poor, free and slave, to receive a mark on his right hand or on his forehead, so that no one could buy or sell unless he had the mark, which is the name of the beast or the number of his name. This calls for wisdom. If anyone has insight, let him calculate the number of the beast, for it is man's number. His number is 666." Notice, you can receive this mark either in your forehead (intelligently, with understanding), or just in your hand (in action, going along with the crowd). Apparently it's not a visible mark, like a brand, but it's still a clear identifying factor.

"God's Seal" or the "Mark"

We've taken a look at the beast. Now, what about this "mark"? If you study Revelation, you discover it revolves around two contrasting symbols—the mark of the beast and the seal of God.

The seal of God, which we've already noticed, represents God's people being settled and unmovable. God is the great developer in the dark room (remember, we don't develop ourselves), and He's looking for the image of Jesus to come out. Then He puts us in the "fixing chemical," and we're set fast.

Along with this is an interesting symbol, called the Sabbath. Where did the Sabbath come from? It came from Eden, as a memorial of creation. Some people think it came from father Abraham. No way! It began hundreds of years earlier. And the "Sabbath was made for man", not just for the Jews. It was made for all mankind, originally for one purpose—to bring glory and honor to the Creator. (When was the last time you stopped and thought about your Creator...stopped to ponder the wonder and the mystery of life...stopped to honor the One who keeps your heart beating every moment?) Apparently the Creator saw that it was good and healthy for people to remember where they came from. So, right there at the very beginning, He rested on the seventh day, and set it aside as a special day to honor creation and the Creator. Thus, the seventh day became a weekly reminder of the birthday of the world, if you please. And if you trace it back, calendar wise, you'll find that the weekly cycle has never been broken, as far back as human records go.

Think about that for a moment. There's an astronomical reason for the year (the earth traveling around the sun). There's an astronomical reason for the day (the earth turning on its axis). There's even an astronomical reason for the month (the relationship of the earth to the moon). But there's only one reason for the week, and that is creation. Even an atheist who says, "Monday is the second day of the week" admits creation in spite of himself by recognizing the weekly cycle.

Changing Times and Laws

Enormous glory and honor belong to the Creator. Scripture says, "Remember your Creator"—and the devil hates it! After his fall from Heaven, he was smarting, so he tried to figure out a way to insult the Creator, the very One who was keeping him alive. He decided that warping God's calendar would divert attention from Him. And hundreds of years before it happened, prophecy predicted a power would arise to assist this scheme. "He will speak against the Most High and oppress his saints, and try to change the set times and the laws." Daniel 7:25. This new power couldn't actually *do* it, but he would *think* he could. That's the literal translation of this passage—"think to."

Suppose I called you and said, "When's your birthday?" You say, "My birthday is August 20." And I say, "We're going to change it to January 1, and start the year with a celebration!" You'd probably say, "Man, you're crazy! No one can change anyone's birthday. God Himself can't change the day I was born on." (I guess they tried with Washington and Lincoln, but that didn't *really* change the day they were born. It just combined holidays for convenience.) And, when you think about it, changing the day you celebrate someone's birthday means the event really doesn't mean the same thing anymore.

(Did you really spend last Presidents' Day reflecting on the freedoms we enjoy because of Washington and Lincoln, and honoring them?)

It's impossible to change God's laws, impossible to change the birthday of the world, but this power "thought" to do it. And according to history, the Catholic Church attempted to change God's day of worship from Saturday to Sunday.

Now, I didn't just dream this up (and neither did anyone else). Catholic fathers and Catholic leaders and Catholic writers have all acknowledged this for a long, long time. If you've read Cardinal Gibbons, Faith of Our Fathers, and other Catholic sources (including the catechisms), you know that they claim that the Catholic Church changed God's day of worship from Saturday to Sunday. They consider this act a "*mark* of their ecclesiastical authority." And just about all the Christian world agrees (at least through their actions), since they follow the Catholics lead in this.

Rationalizing the Change

Now, in order to get the heat off the Catholics during the counter reformation, the Jesuits had to come up with a completely different interpretation of prophecy—to counter the one Martin Luther and other reformers had given. As a result, most Protestants today think that the reason they go to church on Sunday is because of the resurrection.

Actually, I've documented twenty-two different reasons why people go to church on Sunday, and the best *sounding* one is "to honor the resurrection." Unfortunately, it doesn't happen to be Biblical! There's nothing in the Bible about going to church on Sunday to honor the resurrection—not one text. There are a lot of lesser reasons people give (like the disciples took an offering on the first day of the week, and someone else had a meeting on the first day of the week, etc.), but these sound more like excuses.

The *real* reason behind Sunday worship, (if you're wide awake to

Scriptural prophecy) is the very one the Catholics give. (And the reason Protestants who have their eyes and ears objectively open have been embarrassed by Catholics for a long time.) The Catholic Church says to Protestants, "We worship on Sunday because we changed the day from Saturday. Why do you Protestants go to church on Sunday? It's really because the Catholic church gave you that institution. Fine! Then why don't you go along with the rest of our Catholic institutions?" And you've got to admit, that's a worthwhile argument.

Now, for those of you who may wonder about your own practice until now, as well as your sincere relatives from the past, there's an interesting Bible principle that addresses this. It's found in Acts 17:30: "In the past God overlooked such ignorance, but now he commands all people everywhere to repent."

This means mercy for my Grandpa Nels, who came over from Norway with his brothers Knute and Ole—all good Lutherans. And mercy for Christians of past generations who observed Sunday, thinking that they were keeping the Bible Sabbath. And there are true Christians in every church today (even Roman Catholic) who honestly believe that Sunday is the Sabbath of divine appointment. God accepts their sincerity of purpose and their integrity for Him.

But, when Sunday observance shall be enforced by law, and the world is enlightened concerning the true Sabbath, then anyone who transgresses the command of God to obey a precept with no higher authority than Rome will thereby honor popery above God. (And pay homage to the power that enforces the institution ordained by Rome...and worship the beast and his image.) As men then reject the institution which is God's sign of His authority, and honor in its stead that which Rome has chosen as a token of her supremacy, they thereby accept the sign of allegiance to Rome—the mark of the beast.

Notice, it's not until the issue is plainly set before the people, and they must choose between the commandments of God and commandments of men, that those who continue in transgression will receive the mark of the beast.

Standing Firm

So, when does someone receive the mark of the beast? This is how it will work, as I understand it:

The image of the beast is already being set up by Protestant America going bad, reaching over to Rome even as we speak. The stage is being set. Soon there will be global crises, as the angels finally let go the winds, bringing our planet to its knees. Then, the world's leading power, the United States of America, will try to save the Earth from annihilation by inviting Rome to step in. Thus the religious/political combination of the Dark Ages will be resurrected. Persecution will result, and you and I will have two choices— just two.

One, we can go along with the crowd. We'll accept the mark of the beast when it becomes law. We'll be forced to give up any ideas of God's day being sacred, a day in honor of creation—but we'll still be able to buy and sell at Safeway and Albertsons. And, when things heat up, we'll escape the death penalty. Of course, we'll also suffer the seven last plagues and eternal death (after going into the lake of fire with the devil and his angels). Anyone interested?

On the other hand, when the whole world panics and tries to force everyone to worship the same, to keep holy the first day of the week (which was changed as predicted by prophecy), we can say, "Not so. Check your Bibles." And we can stand true to our conscience and conviction concerning our worship of the Creator, and face the threat of persecution. We'll also have something we can hold in our hearts: "He who dwells in the shelter of the Most High will rest in the shadow of the Almighty. I will say of the Lord, 'He is my refuge and my fortress, my God, in whom I trust.' Surely he will save you from the fowler's snare and from the deadly pestilence. He will cover you with his feathers, and under his wings you will find refuge; his faithfulness will be your shield and rampart. You will not fear the terror of night, nor the arrow that flies by day." And right in the middle of Psalms 91 is a promise: "There shall no evil befall thee, neither shall any *plague* come nigh thy dwelling." (KJV) And we'll have the opportunity to rise to the faith of our fathers who sought for freedom, and of having the God who honors freedom as our Father forever.

Depending on the Creator

Well, what about all those hard phrases in Revelation 14? "He will be tormented with burning sulfur in the presence of the holy angels and of the Lamb." Is God into barbecues? Does He like to see people be tormented and burned? Or is there a spiritual principle here?

There's an interesting text in Matthew. "When he arrived at...the region of the Gadarenes, two demon-possessed men coming from the tombs met him...'What do you want with us, Son of God?' they shouted. 'Have you come here to torture us before the appointed time?'" (Matthew 8:29). The presence of the Godly is always torment to the ungodly. Look at the spiritual significance here. People who aren't into spiritual things always have the fidgets around those who are. "And the smoke of their torment rises for ever and ever." Check your Bible, and you'll find this means as long as they live. Anyone dependent on himself (self-made men love to worship their makers), who finds himself in the presence of those giving glory and honor and homage to the Creator, will be in torment.

And then it says, "There is no rest day or night for those who worship the beast and his image." It doesn't say "they shall have no rest day or night." It says they *have* no rest. Those who depend upon themselves, instead of God (which is what the beast and his image is all about), have no rest day or night *right now.*

There's a common thread running through all the angels' messages in Revelation 14. It's the warning against self-worship and trying to save ourselves. Remember, Babylon goes back to Babel, the ancestor of people trying to save themselves. I'm embarrassed to admit how many years I thought the way to be a Christian was to *try hard* to live a good life. I should have known better, but I'd picked this idea up somewhere along the way, from home, or school, or at church. And so I tried very hard for a long time to live a good life.

But, that's the image to the beast—trying to enforce religious duty by human power. (It's the temptation of January 1st. Righteousness by resolution!) Combining religious and human power doesn't work, it never has! The only way we'll ever find relief from having no rest day or night, (now, or anytime we're apart from Jesus) is to accept His invitation, "Come to me, all you who are weary and burdened, and I will give you rest." When we realize we can't save ourselves *in any way* (justification, sanctification, or glorification), then we've gotten victory over the beast and his image and his mark, ahead of time.

Examining Our Priorities

I invite you to develop a personal relationship and dependence upon Jesus. I invite you to get the victory over the beast and his image *today*, so you won't receive the mark tomorrow. I invite you to spend as much time with your Bible and in prayer as you do watching TV. (What? Too big an order? All right, let's make it easier. Just don't spend *more* time watching TV than you spend in devotions.) I invite you, like Jesus did in John 6, to spend as much time seeking Him and learning to depend on Him as you do eating your meals.

We should have realized long ago how healthful it can be to spend a thoughtful hour each day contemplating the life of Christ. Jesus isn't a fanatic. He's not asking the impossible. He doesn't ask you to become some kind of a hermit. He just asks for top priority in your day, so you can walk together, and fellowship together, and get the victory over the beast and his image right now.

And is that really asking too much from the One who loves us, who cares for us, and who died for us so that we might live forever?

Chapter Thirteen

The Time of TROUBLE

Here's a question for all the men. How you would feel if you discovered you were going to have a baby? No, not your wife—you yourself! Now, don't think I'm being overly spectacular here, because this is in your Bible.

I've never had a baby (although I had a kidney stone once, and I *felt* like I was having one!) But imagine, men, what it would be like to be nine months along and facing child-birth. This extreme analogy is what Jeremiah uses to illustrate a big time of trouble ahead.

What about these times of trouble predicted in Scripture? Should we be frightened? Are they good times, or bad times? How do we face the situation? Actually, there are *three* times of trouble, two of them quite obvious in Scripture; the third one alluded to by Jesus.

First, let's turn to Daniel, the 12th chapter, where we find a time of trouble "such as has not happened from the beginning of nations." As you know, Daniel gives the history of the world from about 600 B.C. until the end of time. Close to the end of the book (after some good bedtime stories like the fiery furnace and the lion's den *and* some major lines of prophecy) you come to the moment when, "Michael [also known as Christ], the great prince who protects your people, will arise." (Don't miss that line, "your people," for "If you belong to

Christ, then you are Abraham's seed..." Galatians 3:29) Michael stands up, and then what happens? "There will be a time of distress such as has not happened from the beginning of nations until then. But at that time your people—everyone whose name is found written in the book—will be delivered." (Daniel 12:1)

This time of trouble is very clear. We're told that when Christ stands up, He also lays down a censor, which represents a particular phase of ministry He's been doing in the heavenly country. It also suggests something later made clear (in Revelation 22:11), that there's a final decree made at some point in this world's history—"Let him who does wrong continue to do wrong; let him who is vile continue to be vile; let him who does right continue to do right; and let him who is holy continue to be holy." Our time for decision is finished.

Probation Closes

We might call this time "the close of probation." Now some people panic over that concept, but the close of probation is nothing new. When people die in accidents, their probation closes. It just means things are settled, permanently. There's no second chance. (Of course, the devil is always trying to add a second chance, through gimmicks like reincarnation, in a constant effort to get people to procrastinate and delay a decision.) But that moment in history when the close of probation takes place means we've had our opportunity, and what we've decided is decided, what's settled is settled.

We could become so panicked over the close of probation that we'd forget that it's also *good* news! One afternoon I was at a meeting where people were discussing last day events. Someone with nostrils flaring, their eyes wide with fright, jumped up and said, "What about the close of probation?" And someone else responded, "Well, when it closes, we won't be on probation anymore." I like that!

But there's a note of finality about the close of probation. As we read Daniel and Revelation together, we see that right after this Daniel 12 statement come the seven last plagues of Revelation 16—God's judgments upon the earth, and the great time of trouble. We'll study more about that later on.

Another Time of Trouble

Let's look at a second time of trouble. This one is in Jeremiah (where we'll find out about this men having babies thing!) "Can a man bear children? Then why do I see every strong man with his hands on his stomach like a woman in labor, every face turned deathly pale? How awful that day will be! None will be like it. It will be a time of trouble for Jacob..." And don't miss this last line. "...but he shall be saved out of it." (Jeremiah 30:6-7)

What an interesting way to describe big trouble. God's people will apparently go through something similar to Jacob's experience when he got in a wrestling match with Jesus by the brook Jabbok. Do you remember the story? As he's returning home from exile, Jacob finds out that Esau, still angry, is out to get him. Jacob divides his company and goes to spend the night praying by the brook. A hand is placed upon him. He thinks it's an enemy. And the fight begins.

Sometimes when God's hand is placed on us, we think it's an enemy. Sometimes, just like Jacob, we get into a fight with Jesus, until the day breaks and the light dawns. Apparently there's something about Jacob's experience that's going to happen to God's people before this world is over. During the great time of trouble, after the close of probation, God's people experience some kind of desperate struggle.

So you have these two times of trouble: The great time of trouble such as never was, and during a part of that time, the time of Jacob's trouble (that's purely for God's people).

Trouble Number Three

But there's a third time of trouble. Let's go back to the year 1847, shortly after the great disappointment of 1844 when thousands thought Jesus was returning to end the sinful world. William Miller, a Baptist farmer turned preacher, had three thousand other preachers join him in tracing down the lines of Bible prophecy in Daniel and Revelation. They came to the conclusion that the world would end on October 22, 1844. When it didn't happen, there were many people who turned their backs on God and faith. They had nothing more to do with religion at all, calling it a big hoax.

But there were other people who said, "We can't deny what we've studied. We've felt the presence of God , and we'll continue to study until we understand what's going on." And they did. As time passed, they discovered what really began on October 22. They also began to discover related truths they'd never noticed before. They found that the seventh-day Sabbath was not given to the Jews (it went clear back to creation), and that God had given it as a weekly reminder of the Creator. At first that didn't seem like a big deal. But as they studied the prophecies of Daniel and Revelation, they found out how deeply God feels about this day, and how the devil has tried to undermine it. So they began to teach it.

About this time they began to see a fulfillment of the prophecy of Joel, referred to on the day of Pentecost by Peter. Visions and dreams were given by God to encourage the little group. The gift of prophecy began to be made manifest. (Remember, this wasn't a denomination. People from all different faiths were involved. They were a kind of loosely-knit mystical church, comprised of people desperately serious about the things of God.) And they listened with intense interest to these messages from God.

Here's something that was envisioned in 1847: "At the commencement of the time of trouble, we were filled with the Holy Spirit as we went forth and proclaimed the Sabbath more fully."

Evidently in this vision, probation's door is still open so people can hear and accept truth. And it talks about a time of trouble that apparently takes place before the close of probation. Sometime later the author gave this explanation: "This view was given...when there were but very few of the Advent people observing the Sabbath. And of these but few supposed that its observance was of sufficient importance. Now the fulfillment of that view is beginning to be seen. The commencement of that time of trouble here mentioned does not refer to the time when the plagues shall begin to be poured out, but to a short period, just before they are poured out. At that time, while the work of salvation is closing, trouble will be coming on the earth and the nations will be angry, yet held in check so as not to prevent the work of the three angels of Revelation 14. At that time the latter rain, or refreshing from the presence of the Lord, will come to give power to the loud cry of the third angel and prepare the saints to stand in the period when the seven last plagues shall be poured out."

So, as we put this all together, we see that before the close of probation there's a mighty power attending the message that's being presented by people trying to reach others who haven't heard. And it comes at the commencement of a time of trouble. This might be called the "little time of trouble" or "the early time of trouble."

More About Probation

Now we need to discuss the two closes of probation. Two? That's right. Perhaps you remember the polarization process we mentioned earlier. Before Jesus comes, everyone is going to go one way or the other. (You probably know which way you're going right now—whether you're becoming warmer and warmer concerning the things of God, or colder and colder.) Everyone goes through this polarization. And eventually all the lukewarm people disappear.

Apparently those who've had the opportunity to understand light and truth concerning Christ's righteousness instead of their own, and how it's revealed in the three angels' messages (Revelation 14), will have their probation closed before the rest of the world.

Here again is inside information from yesteryear concerning that. "Oh that the people might know the time of their visitation! There are many who have not yet heard truth for this time. There are many with whom the Spirit of God is striving. The time of God's destructive judgments is the time of mercy for those who had no opportunity to learn what is truth."

This can't be talking about the destructive judgment of the seven last plagues *after* the close of probation. Apparently the angels are beginning to loosen up, and winds are beginning to blow, a short time before the close of probation. Perhaps we can see this shaping up, even now, in natural disasters and angry nations. As God's destructive judgments begin, there's still time for those who've had no opportunity to learn truth. God will look tenderly upon these people, His heart of mercy touched. His hand will stretch out to save them, even while the door is closed to those who wouldn't enter.

A Time of Great Trouble

O.K. Let's piece together what we've learned thus far. We see a people emerging who know what is true, and who have a message for this time. They're the ones left after the shake-up, after everyone's relationship with God goes one way or the other. These people move out with great power (under what's called the loud cry and the latter rain), and other people who haven't heard this message respond before the close of probation.

But the success attending this outpouring of the Spirit makes the "religious right" angry since it doesn't fit their plans. And real trouble begins—BIG trouble! In the midst of global crises, and calamities throughout the world, fierce opposition (even persecution) will begin to rise against God's people. And trouble surrounds them.

Now if you carefully study the times of trouble as revealed in Scripture, you'll discover some interesting insights. Let's examine some of these in the next few paragraphs.

First, every soul must stand for himself before God during that time. Apparently it's not a family thing. No one is going to slide through on Father's or Mother's coattail. It's every one for himself.

Second, evil angels will exercise destructive power during this time. But, following the close of probation, the devil can't destroy God's people, even during this great time of trouble.

Third, it will require a faith that can endure weariness, hunger, and delay. It will be a fearful ordeal for God's people.

Also, during this time, God's people will be fleeing from the cities and towns, fleeing from infuriated mobs. This is going to be an even greater crisis than God's people anticipate.

Preparing for the Troubles

But God's people don't need to make provision for temporal needs or wants during the time of trouble. A few years ago I visited some people in the mountains who'd made just such a plan. I couldn't believe the mansion they'd designed to survive the time of trouble. Someone recently told me about a place they bought in Montana. And now, they've added to their possessions even more by purchasing another, even more isolated place.

Thinking of this reminded me about what's stored in my garage. When we moved to our present home five years ago, we bought a house that had a garage filled with something the owner had paid hundreds of dollars to get. Disaster provisions! Cases and boxes of dried food and dried powdered milk and everything else. It was all out there. Now they were moving and they didn't know what to do with it all. So I said, "Just leave it there." I guess I figured I might use it during the times of trouble. But it had already been there fifteen years when we bought the place—so now I have cases and cases of *twenty-year-old powered milk*! When it comes to making material provisions for the time of trouble, forget it! It's a waste of time.

A Look at Martyrs

Well, what about that word persecution? Will there be martyrs? Are the persecutions of the Dark Ages going to be revived? If so, should that frighten us? When I began studying this, I decided to spend some time reading about the martyrs.

I wonder if anyone today is interested in *being* a martyr. Do you realize that all Jesus' disciples, except one, *were* martyrs? In addition, the Apostle Paul, who wrote fourteen New Testament books, was beheaded. And John the Baptist (of whom Jesus said, "there is no one greater than John") was beheaded, alone, in a dungeon.

Not long ago I heard a pastor from the Middle East give a personal witness. They don't have the kind of freedoms we have in the United States. He'd been in situations where there was hardly one chance in a thousand he'd come out alive. And God always brought him through. But the impressive thing was that God gave him peace, *absolute peace,* throughout the entire ordeal.

I heard someone say, "Oh martyrdom! That's no big deal." I thought he was being pretty flippant about it, until I began to understand what he was saying. "Blessed are those who are persecuted because of righteousness." (Matthew 5:10) There's a blessing promised here. (And I hope I'd be able to accept the experience as well as the theory.) Jesus told us not to be afraid of those who could kill our bodies—be afraid of those who can kill our souls. So, I guess Jesus Himself was saying, "When it comes to martyrdom, it's no big deal."

Then, as I continued to search God's Word, I realized that the Apostle Paul *rejoiced* to suffer for Christ's sake. The martyrs actually *praised*

God for the opportunity to join Jesus in that kind of testimony.

In the time prior to the last closing conflict, many may be imprisoned, many may flee for their lives from cities and towns, and many may even be martyred for Christ's sake while standing in defense of what is true. But God has promised that we will not be tempted above what we can bear. And Jesus bore all of this, and more, for us.

Speaking of promises, John gives us a glimpse of how God plans to treat these martyrs (Revelation 20:4). It's right there in the middle of the millennium passage. "I saw thrones on which were seated those who had been given authority to judge. And I saw the souls of those who had been beheaded because of their testimony for Jesus and because of the word of God. They had not worshiped the beast or his image and had not received his mark on their foreheads or their hands. [And] they...reigned with Christ..."

Strength for the Hour

Here's a point worth noting: The courage and the fortitude of the martyrs is not given to anyone *until it's needed.* So don't read your children bedtime stories from Fox's book of martyrs! (And don't dwell on it yourself, either.) Thinking about the possibilities could panic even the most godly person in the world, because the courage to meet the situation hasn't been supplied yet. Which is just another way of saying, "Martyrdom is no big deal *when it comes*."

Even the disciples were not endowed with the courage and the fortitude of martyrs until such grace was needed. (In fact, during an earlier crisis, they took to their heels!) But when it was needed, the Savior's promise was fulfilled.

The simple reality is that we won't be able to meet *any* of the coming trials without God's power. (If you're a stubborn Dutchman, you might be able to endure some things on backbone alone, but not the time of trouble.) But then, we're not *expected* to have the courage and fortitude of the martyrs of old *until* we're brought into the position they were in. In the meantime, we're to receive daily supplies of grace to meet each daily emergency. And thus we grow in the grace and the knowledge of our Lord Jesus Christ, and if persecution comes and we're enclosed in prison walls for faith in Jesus and keeping His commandments, then "as thy days, so shall thy strength be."

I've heard some people get a sort of "martyr thrill syndrome" and feel sure they'd be on the right side. "If I lived back in the days of Huss and Jerome and Latimer and Cranmer," they say, "I'd just step forward and say, 'Go ahead, burn me!'" Some people like the thrill of thinking the blood of martyrs courses through their veins. But the only people who will go through the times *ahead* are the ones who are getting closer to Jesus *now.* And then the real heroes will show up.

I always love to read about Huss and Jerome. Huss was taken to the stake and never flinched. Jerome, his friend, flinched. He became fearful. He recanted his faith—but then he discovered that it's harder to live without Christ than to die for Him. Back to the prelates he went, and said, "I want to recant my recantation!" He told of his remorse in turning his back on Jesus. So they hurried him out to the stake where they had prepared a slow fire with green wood. They put the devil cap on his head and committed his soul to the devil. And as the flames slowly began to rise, he took his right hand (with which he had signed the recantation) and thrust it in the flames first. That's the way he wanted it. Then he, like his friend Huss, died singing hymns.

Now, the last time I put my hand on a hot stove I did *not* sing hymns! Which means there's some kind of miracle going on here. What is that miracle? The courage and fortitude of the martyrs that comes from God at the very time it's needed most. Which leads me to conclude with this premise:

The *greatest* time of trouble is to be without Jesus then...or now!

Chapter Fourteen

Seven Last PLAGUES

It's a topic that has troubled people for a long time. We've read about it, and we've wondered. The seven last plagues almost seem like a sort of vegetarian hell-fire—just another way to scare people into obeying. I know I felt that way in the past.

There are a lot of different ideas floating around about this topic. Some people say that the plagues aren't literal, they're only symbolic. Some say that God brings them; others say the devil brings them; still others say we bring them on ourselves.

And some people, these days, even try to ignore the plagues. I mean, how can we get a handle on anything so fearful? But you just can't study last day events without running into Revelation 16, and I'm determined not to ignore it in our study together.

Let's begin with a brief overview. One person described the situation this way: "I dreamed of enduring the awful sight of the seven last plagues, the wrath of God. I saw that His anger was dreadful and terrible. And if He should stretch forth His hand or lift it in anger, the inhabitants of the world would be as though they had never been. All would suffer from the incurable sores and withering plagues that would come upon them. And they would find no deliverance, but be destroyed by them. Terror seized me. And I fell upon my face before the angel and begged of him to cause the sight to be removed, to hide it from me because it was too dreadful." (Somebody press the stop button, please!) "Then I realized, as many before, the importance of searching the Word of God carefully to know how to escape the plagues, which that Word declares shall come on all the ungodly who shall worship the beast and his image. It was a great wonder for me that any could transgress the law of God when such awful threatenings and denunciations were against them."

So, what do we do with these seven last plagues? Do we treat them like other promises in Scripture? Do we memorize them? Or put them on the visor in our car? Or hang them over the sink where we wash the dishes?

The First Five Plagues

Let's look at the first five of these plagues found in Revelation 16. It's our understanding that they occur during "the time of trouble such as never was", *after* Daniel 12:1 has been fulfilled, and *after* the statement that whoever is holy stays holy, and whoever is filthy remains filthy. Michael stands up. Probation has closed and all hell breaks loose. But all heaven breaks loose too!

So, let's read what Scripture describes in Revelation 16:1-11. "Then I heard a loud voice from the temple saying to the seven angels, 'Go, pour out the seven bowls of God's wrath on the earth.' The first angel went and poured out his bowl on the land, and ugly and painful sores broke out on the people who had the mark of the beast and worshiped his image. The second angel poured out his bowl on the sea, and it turned into blood like that of a dead man, and every living thing in the sea died. The third angel poured out his bowl on the rivers and springs of water, and they became blood."

Now, right here we have a statement made by the angels (which is due about this time): "Then I heard the angel in charge of the waters say: 'You are just in these judgments, you who are and who were, the Holy One, because you have so judged; for they have shed the blood of your saints and prophets, and you have given them blood to drink as they deserve.' And I heard the alter respond: 'Yes, Lord God Almighty, true and just are your judgments.'"

So, if anyone has any questions about God's judgments and what is happening, the angels themselves agree that it's fair. "The fourth angel poured out his bowl on the sun, and the sun was given power to scorch people with fire. They were seared by the intense heat and they cursed the name of God, who had control over these plagues, but they refused to repent and glorify him. The fifth angel poured out his bowl on the throne of the beast, and his kingdom was plunged into darkness. Men gnawed their tongues in agony and cursed the God of heaven because of their pains and their sores, but they refused to repent of what they had done." You have to admit that this is a time of genuine turmoil.

Plagues as Discipline?

Now I'm taking the position (but remember, don't believe what anyone *says*—study it out for yourself!) that these plagues are literal, not symbolic, and that they're brought by God, not the devil. You see, if they were brought by the devil, then I would have to conclude that God and the devil are partners, do business together, and are probably good friends—which wasn't the case the last I heard!

"Well," someone asks, "why do these plagues come? Are they for discipline?" There's evidence in Scripture that Egypt's ten plagues came for disciplinary purposes—so people would wake up, see their errors, and change. But when the seven last plagues arrive, it's too late to change. Why would you give bloodthirsty people an overdose of blood (with the hope that this treatment would change them) when it's *already too late* to change?

Back when we were teenagers, there was a store in town with a soda fountain. The man who ran it took a special interest in us teens. One day he made us an offer. He said, "Come on over, and I'll give you five milkshakes a piece. If you drink all five, you can have them free. But if you don't drink all five, you have to pay for whatever you drink." So, greedy teenagers that we were, we jumped in a car and went down there. As we drank away on these huge milkshakes, he watched our faces. He kept putting in those rich ingredients; we kept pigging out. Most of us made it through part of the fourth one—before we wished we were dead! He made a lot of money that day, and we lost interest in milkshakes for a long, long time. It was sort of a disciplinary thing. (And, I'm not sure, but perhaps he made a point that day about the need for temperance, too!)

Anyway, giving people an overdose of blood because they're bloodthirsty, with the idea they're going to change, is rather senseless if probation has closed and people are already set in cement! The wicked are wicked forever (for the rest of their existence, if you please), and the righteous are righteous forever. It's all over—so you can't chalk the plagues up as disciplinary, because it's too late for discipline.

Plagues as Revenge?

"Oh," you say, "then the seven last plagues and the end fires must have to do with getting even." Some of us can go for that. You may have read the story, in the papers a few years ago, about the little girl in Madera, California, who was spanked by her father. She didn't cry, so he continued to beat her. He kept at it for half an hour, trying to make her cry, until she finally asked if she could have a glass of water. And then she died.

When I read that story, I said to myself, "Death is too good for that man! He needs the same kind of treatment." That's how my mind works. But, then I read Romans 12:19: "Do not take revenge, my friends, but leave room for God's wrath, for it is written: 'It is mine to avenge; I will repay,' says the Lord." So, Scripture says vengeance belongs to God. He knows what's what, and He will repay. (That old "eye for an eye, and tooth for a tooth" concept that Moses laid out sounds pretty good sometimes, but Jesus exemplified a whole new approach for us to follow in the New Testament.)

Is God really like me when it comes to relating to that father and that little girl? Do I really *want* Him to be like me? Is God going to avenge someday? Not, apparently, for the purpose of winning the hearts of the wicked, because it's too late for that. And even if it wasn't too late, that has never been God's method.

Listen! It is not (and never has been) part of Christ's mission to *force* us to receive Him. It's Satan, (and those actuated by his spirit) who seeks to *compel* the conscience. Such men (pretending a zeal for righteousness, but in reality, aligned with evil angels) bring suffering on others in order to "convert" them to their ideas of religion. But Christ ever shows mercy, ever seeks to win by revealing of His love. He wants no rival in our souls, will not accept partial service—but He desires only *voluntary* service, the willing surrender of our hearts to the constraint of love. There's no more conclusive evidence that we possess the spirit of Satan than the disposition to hurt or destroy those who don't appreciate our work, or who act contrary to our ideas!

This includes Pat Robertson and the religious right. This includes the Pope. And this includes you and me, and our relationship to each other and our church. But does it include God? Will God operate like Satan in the end? Or could it be that there's some other issue involved in these seven last plagues—that perhaps God isn't just trying to hurt somebody because they didn't agree with Him?

Scripture says God has no pleasure in the death of the wicked and it calls the judgment, "His strange act." Why? Because we have no idea of the mercy and patience and long-suffering of God. Go back to the Old Testament and notice the hundreds and hundreds of years that God was patient with His people as they went up and down, back and forth—now worshiping idols, then serving God for a short time, now down to lower depths again with idols. It went on for centuries! And we've seen Jesus' patience with people like Judas—and Peter.

God is known for His enduring mercy. Perhaps that's why the Bible calls the judgment a strange act, and why even the angels might have questions. But then, the angels unite in chorus to say, "True and just are your ways." Why? Because God is true to His Word. He's warned us that the seven last plagues will fall on those who worship the beast and his image, and He'll keep His word.

Of course there's the old saying, "the punishment fits the crime." But what's the point of punishment now? And is that what the seven last plagues are all about—punishment?

Some Comparisons

Here's where comparing the plagues of Egypt and the seven last plagues might prove helpful.

First point: *God's power and authority are supreme.* Both the plagues of Egypt and the seven last plagues demonstrate this. You have people among the wicked who are atheists, who believe man came from another source, who don't believe God exists, who (in Egypt's day) worship the river and the frogs. Suddenly they can no longer deny there's a bigger power, a larger authority. Supernatural events become a testimony to God's superior power and authority.

Point Two: *The enemy is defeated.* The end result of the plagues is the defeat of the rebel. Just as it happened in Egypt with Pharoah, it will happen at the end of time with Satan.

Point Three: *God's people are delivered.* This was the objective in Egypt, and it's a primary goal during the ominous time of the plagues. Why? Because condemnation and persecution by the majority apparently put God's people under tremendous pressure.

As in the plagues of Egypt, the seven last plagues demonstrate

God's justice even as they occur. If my son is beating my daughter, then I'm not a father of love unless I do something about it (whether it's discipline or not). So when God's people are under the death penalty, and being persecuted, and running for their lives, then perhaps it's not at all wrong for God to give the wicked something else to think about (like blood for water)—something to distract them from their evil designs. In effect, God is saying, "If you're content spending your time trying to figure out a way to destroy My people, then here's something else for you to think about!"

And here's an interesting point. The plagues all seem to relate to present issues, issues very relevant to the situation. The Egyptians worshiped the Nile River. But in essence, the Nile turned on them. They also worshiped frogs. But the frogs turned on them, too. And thus, the futility of relying on false gods became very clear.

Notice, the first of the seven last plagues (ugly and painful sores) falls on those who worship the beast and his image. It's obvious that the group that has chosen this route is in for a rough ride!

Plagues two and three revolve around people who seem intent on shedding blood, and forcing people to believe the way they believe. They're totally bloodthirsty, so they're given blood to drink. (You want blood? Here's an overdose!)

Plague number four has to do with the sun. For centuries people have worshiped the sun. In fact, a day of worship was established in honor of the sun, and its name, "Sun's day," has come down to us from ancient paganism. This false day of worship will be very much on people's minds during this time. (We've already discussed how our allegiance is related to this issue—God's day or the counterfeit day.) Suddenly, people will discover that allegiance to Sun's day is not going to help them at all. In fact, the sun will scorch them with intense heat! (You want sun. Here's plenty of sun!)

Interested in a sunburn? No thanks! We took off down river, one vacation, on a three-day raft trip—high school teens, we were going to do the Huckleberry Finn thing. We'd built a raft, ten feet by twelve.

We had a fifty gallon drum in each corner, and wall-to-wall carpet, and a little tent pitched in the middle. So we started off down river taking turns at navigating, and reading, and looking at the scenery. It was a beautiful, sunny day. But it wasn't long until we discovered what the sun can do. By evening, we were in big trouble—talk about your sunburn! We crawled painfully onto the shore. One of our group stumbled across a plowed field to a farmhouse and called his father, who was an undertaker, for help. He came out and picked us up—in the hearse! We wished we'd never *seen* the sun!

The sun can be friendly. But when this time in earth's history arrives (as predicted in prophecy), it will mean everything if we can claim the promise of Psalm 91, "He who dwells in the shelter of the Most High will rest in the *shadow* of the Almighty."

Now during this sun plague, people begin to blame God (just as they did in Egypt's plagues). Atheists, who "don't believe in God," blame *God!* Infidels, and skeptics, and cynics, and agnostics blame God. Suddenly they realize they're fighting against someone bigger than themselves. There is a God after all! And then, they begin to blame God's people for all the trouble! Proud and stubborn, they're susceptible to neither Divine mercy *nor severity!* Interesting!

You may have noticed that days of hurt and pain often seem to accomplish what ease and blessing do not. People who would never respond under ease may turn to God under trouble. Although few such "deathbed repentances" seem to last, there's at least a synthetic repentance for a time (such as with Judas or Pharaoh). But not so in this case! Scripture says these people are so polarized against God that not only are they wicked and rebellious, but they also blaspheme the name of God as well. In the eyes of the universe, (the jury looking on) it becomes crystal clear just how set wickedness really is.

Then comes the fifth plague—darkness. What's wrong with that? We can all enjoy the night. But evidently this is a different kind of darkness—so thick it can be cut. The kind of darkness that brings the deepest panic. People gnaw their tongues in agony over the sores and the blood and the heat *and the darkness*—utter darkness for those who have chosen darkness over light. An overdose of darkness! All the gods that people have served now turn on them. And suddenly they realize there's someone superior in charge somewhere. But they *still* refuse to repent and give Him the glory. That's what it says.

Plagues as a Revelation

Now, I believe God knows His business, and He doesn't do anything that's not necessary. And so, the plagues have a proper place. Let me suggest a couple of possible functions.

First, to reveal that it's God Himself the rebels have been fighting. All must acknowledge God, regardless of their position.

Second, to reveal that these rebels have no repentance of any kind—to show that the wicked are just as sealed as the righteous, and that ultimate polarization has taken place. The tares are shown to be super tares; the wheat, to be super wheat. Thus the stage is set for God's justice in allowing the wicked to be destroyed. Scripture says that before everything is finished, every knee will bow and confess that God is just and fair. And apparently, that's the purpose of this time in earth's history.

But something fascinating is happening here. These two groups are so polarized that they're now complete opposites! One group, the righteous, are willing to die because they love. The other group, the wicked, are willing to kill because they hate.

It's ironic that former lukewarm church members will be right in there cursing God alongside Hitler and Hussein. (God forgive me for judging.) The most reprobate, most blasphemous—screaming their heads off at God—will apparently be joined by that little lukewarm church member who was just "too busy" to find time for God. They will all curse and blaspheme God together. Explain that one!

Perhaps we've already seen a sample of this. If I'm too busy to have time for God, but claim to be a Christian and hope to be in His kingdom, then I'm expecting to get there some other way. How? Salvation by my own works. But when I find out my works don't cut it, I'm going to be mad. Even today we find irate people discovering (in the righteousness by faith message) that all their hard work doesn't mean a thing. And they're furious when they don't get credit for their good living. It makes lukewarm people red-hot. And someday they will probably blaspheme and scream at God along with all the rest.

The line will be clearly drawn between those who serve God and those who don't. It's like polishing gold in contrast with polishing tinsel. The more the troubles of life and the pressures of "the time of trouble" rub them, the more the righteous will shine—and the more the wicked will flake off and show what they're really made of! It all figures into the picture that develops before the final judgment.

The devil has had his chance to demonstrate what the universe would be like if he were in charge—and *nobody* is interested in *his* program anymore!

Under His Wings

Friend, we must learn to dwell in the "secret place" of the Most High. Do you have a secret place where you go alone with this God who loves you and proved it through Jesus? Do you have a secret place that's more important than anything else in your day? Is spending time there alone with Jesus your top priority? If it is, then you can truly "abide under the shadow of the Almighty", and sing:

"Under His wings I am safely abiding, Though the night deepens and tempests are wild. Still I can trust Him, I know He will keep me. He has redeemed me and I am His child. Under His wings, Under His wings. Who from His love can sever? Under His wings, my soul shall abide. Safely abide forever."[1]

[1] W. O. Cushing

Chapter Fifteen

Jacob's *TROUBLE*

Someone once said, "Money doesn't buy happiness, but it does give you the chance to choose which type of misery you prefer!" And so, it might be said that Jesus doesn't always promise us freedom from trouble, but He does give us (by His grace), the opportunity to choose which kind of trouble we prefer!

Some have wavered under the misunderstanding (concerning these end time events) that they'll be able to avoid trouble by turning their backs on their faith and on God. No way! This is hardly a solution. If I try to get out of trouble by turning my back on God, then I'm in for even *bigger* trouble. (You already knew that, didn't you?) It's only God's grace that gives us the choice of which kind of trouble we want. And then He promises to walk with us through the right choice. Remember, God didn't deliver Daniel *from* the lion's den—He delivered him *in* the lion's den. He didn't deliver those three faithful Hebrews *from* the fiery furnace—He delivered them *in* it. Do you get the point?

Now, because of His love, He gives us (ahead of time) some video clips of what's coming so we can be better prepared to understand what's going on. And that's why we've included "the time of Jacob's trouble" in our study.

Let's review. We've discussed the close of probation, preceded by what we called the "little time of trouble." This earlier time of trouble is when people try to force others to be good by law. (We might call that "righteousness by force.") Some of God's people will suffer persecution, maybe even martyrdom. But, we're told, this is no reason to fear. Then probation closes and the "great time of trouble such as never was" begins—including the seven last plagues. But God's people don't have to be afraid of that either, because "...You will not fear the terror of night...nor the plague that destroys at midday..." (Psalms 91:5,6) So the "early time of trouble" and the "great time of trouble" are no big deal.

If we're looking for the time that's the *biggest* stress factor, it would have to be "the time of Jacob's trouble". The first five plagues have done their work, the sixth plague enters, and Jacob's trouble begins.

Returning to Eden

"'The days are coming,' declares the Lord, 'when I will bring my people Israel and Judah back from captivity and restore them to the land I gave their forefathers to possess.'" (Jeremiah 30:3) When this passage was first written, undoubtedly the people of Judah and Israel knew it applied to them. But there's a phrase in here that can also apply to Abraham's spiritual seed. You might not have any of Israel's or Judah's blood flowing in your veins, but as Paul said, "If you belong to Christ, then are you Abraham's seed, and heirs according to the promise." This double application puts *you* in the picture.

Now, notice it says God will cause them to return to the land He gave their fathers. What was the land that God gave our father—our original father, Adam? The Garden of Eden. Where's the Garden of Eden now? Some of us believe it's in the Heavenly country. And God has made provision for those who are Christ's to return to this land that was given to their father, and to possess it.

But, before that happens, something else occurs. Look at verse four of this passage: "These are the words the Lord spoke concerning Israel and Judah: 'This is what the Lord says: Cries of fear are heard—terror, not peace. Look and see: Can a man bear children? Then why do I see every strong man with his hands on his stomach like a woman in labor, every face turned deathly pale? How awful that day will be! None will be like it. It will be a time of trouble for Jacob, but he will be saved out of it.'" (Jeremiah 30:4-7) Here we have the time known as "the time of Jacob's trouble," and it happens before we return to the land of our fathers. It's not a time of peace, but a time of turmoil.

What kind of turmoil? What's this trouble all about? And what can God's people expect during this "time of Jacob's trouble"?

Jacob's Story

To help us understand, let's recap the original story of Jacob's trouble. (It's found in Genesis.) Jacob's twin brother, Esau, didn't value the birthright and sold out to Jacob for a kettle of lentils—he didn't realize that you can't barter God's blessing! Years passed and the time came for bestowing the birthright. Esau decided he wanted it after all. So, when old, blind father Isaac asked for venison stew, Esau took off to hunt the ingredients. But, while he was gone, Jacob and mother Rebecca got their heads together. (That was a common thing for this tribe—Abraham made this mistake, too! "God is taking too long on this; we'd better give Him a hand.") "Esau's about to get the birthright," they thought, "so we'd better do something!" They put some fur on Jacob (who was a smooth man), so he could go in to his father and make Isaac think he was Esau (who was a hairy man). Isaac was deceived, and Jacob collected the birthright.

But he also collected a long journey across the desert, fleeing from his irate brother, never to see his mother again. In discouragement, Jacob stretched out on the sand, a rock for a pillow. He thought all was lost. He was guilty of what his name signified—supplanter. He was a deceiver, a cheat, a liar. He felt completely outcast and alone. But, in the middle of the night, he dreamed of a ladder reaching from earth to heaven, representing hope. He woke up and realized that God still knew his address, even though he'd moved to the desert. Jacob vowed he would be God's son, and in the twenty years that followed little heaps of stones were left everywhere he went, representing his times of worship. He was a converted man. He had hope. He had seen the heavenly vision. And he continued to be a genuine follower of God, with worship every morning and evening.

But for twenty years he continued to fight God in ways he didn't understand—just like we do! We may be Christians, may have had our "Jacob's ladder" dream long ago. But we're still fighting God if we think He needs our help with things He's promised to do for us.

Notice, on things God *hasn't* promised to do for us, He *wants* our efforts—and they're very significant! But on things God promises to do *for* us, He doesn't need our help, He doesn't want our help, and our "help" actually hinders His work.

Often we're deeply involved in "the Lord's work." But isn't it about time we stopped trying to do God's work for Him? There are two ways to fight an auto mechanic, you know. My car doesn't work and I say, "I don't need a mechanic." I don't even go to him. That's one way to fight him. The other is more subtle. I go to the mechanic and park my car in his garage. He opens the hood. He begins working in the engine compartment. I poke my head in from the other side and say, "Don't touch the distributor. I put that on new, myself...and stay away from those spark plugs...and don't bother with the fan belt... or the carburetor." After a while he throws down his tools, throws up his hands, and says, "Take it. Fix it yourself if you're so smart!"

For twenty years Jacob kept trying to help God out in various ways. It went back to his experience with his mother. Jacob and Rebecca's problem wasn't so much the lie they told, as the *reason* they told the lie. The problem was in their unsurrendered lives, trying to do what God had promised He would accomplish. The essence of Jesus' teachings was self-surrender; learning what the angels and unfallen worlds already embrace—that we are creatures. We are dependent on someone beside ourselves. Our self-sufficiency and sinful independence are our biggest problems. And learning to depend upon God to do what He has promised (in His own time), is a significant lesson God's people must learn before this world ends.

The Story Continues

Now, back to Jacob. Twenty years have passed. Jacob is finally heading back to the land of his fathers. Suddenly he's told that brother Esau is coming to meet him—with four hundred armed soldiers! And "Jacob was left alone, and a man wrestled with him till daybreak." (Until the breaking of the day. Until the day dawned. Until the lights came on.) "When the man saw that he could not overpower him, he touched the socket of Jacob's hip so that his hip was wrenched as he wrestled with the man. Then the man said, 'Let me go, for it is daybreak.' But Jacob replied, 'I will not let you go unless you bless me.' The man asked him, 'What is your name?' 'Jacob,' (which means liar) he answered. Then the man said, 'Your name will no longer be Jacob, but Israel, because you have struggled with God and with men and have overcome.' Jacob said, 'Please tell me your name.' But he replied, 'Why do you ask my name?'" (That's a polite of saying, "None of your business!") "Then he blessed him there. So Jacob called the place Peniel, saying, 'It is because I saw God face to face, and yet my life was spared.' The sun rose above him as he passed Peniel, and he was limping because of his hip." (Genesis 32:24-32)

Back at camp, as Jacob returned from his night alone, people said, "Who's that coming?" "That's Jacob." "No, that can't be Jacob, he's limping." "Yes, he's been with God." "But you don't limp when you've been with God!" Yes, friend, sometimes you do. Sometimes loving fathers must do things that hurt for a deeper purpose. That's Biblical.

So what's happening here in the experience of Jacob? He heard that his brother was coming with all these soldiers, and so he resorted to his usual strategies. The Pentagon would have been proud of him. He divided his company into two groups, so that if one group got attacked, the other could get away. (And he made sure his favorite wife was in the one that would get away.) He devised a number of different approaches to meet every scenario he could think up. He did everything that was in his power to solve the problem.

Then, finally, he decided to go under the cover of night to pray. (Well, what a novel idea! You mean it's finally come to that?) So he went off to pray. And he was alone. When you come to your Brook Jabbok and your wrestling, you too will be alone. You might be with your family, and you might not, but you'll still be alone. No one will experience the last day events and go back to possess the land of our fathers on someone else's coat-tails. God does not have grandsons and granddaughters—only sons and daughters. And everyone must answer for himself.

God's People Troubled

Well, what makes up the "trouble" part of the time of Jacob's trouble? First, Jacob was genuinely concerned for his family. He was worried that he had brought this emergency upon himself by poor decisions made some twenty years before, and that his loved ones would have to suffer because of it. Once again he was facing the angry brother he'd wronged, and whom he'd fled from years before. And, as I understand it, during this time of Jacob's trouble, God's people will be concerned that they, too, have brought trouble upon themselves by their poor judgment, their lack of sense, in the past. They'll remember many situations and wish they could go back and do things differently.

We also know that Jacob was apparently concerned about the

prospect of torture and death. And God's people, during this time of Jacob's trouble, will be concerned about torture and death, too, because now something totally incredible happens. Satan himself appears, impersonating Christ. All those people who have been campaigning for "righteousness by force" will suddenly get a huge boost to their cause. Satan stages a fake second coming and apparently pulls it off quite well. He's able to maneuver some sort of celestial fireworks, and all across the earth it's shouted that Christ has come again. (If you've been following the New Age movement, you know they're already setting the stage for this scenario.) And in spite of all the fanfare, it's really just the wolf in sheep's clothing!

Satan then takes control, and the world becomes a dictatorship under his rule. Panicked leaders are ready to do exactly what he says. And what does he say? Basically the same thing Caiaphas said a long time ago when faced with the problem of Jesus. Remember how he stood before the council that was deadlocked in confusion and said, "You know nothing at all! Don't you understand that it's better for one man to die than for the whole nation to perish?" And it will be the same at the end. The enemy will convince the whole world that the reason for the troubles, and the calamities, and the natural disasters, and the plagues, is because a group of people have continued to insist on worshiping God by faith instead of by force, worshiping as their conscience tells them instead of the way the law dictates. And as a solution, he says, "Get rid of them!" So a death decree with real teeth in it is passed, and (just like Jacob) the people of God are faced with the prospect of torture and death.

God's people face another concern as well. They're troubled with remorse, and perhaps the remnants of former guilt. Now there's a difference between remorse and guilt. And one of their concerns is that they haven't repented of every sin.

(Some of us grew up with a frightening misconception we picked up somewhere—at home, or school, or church, who knows? It's the idea that if, during the end time, we can remember even one sin, then we're finished, we're history, we're lost forever. And so we find it all too easy to fall into the "righteousness by confession" syndrome—making sure we go over our list of sins, and check it twice each night as we go to bed, even if we fall asleep while we're doing it! After all, we sure don't want one forgotten sin to pop up in our remembrance when the time of trouble comes—or we won't make it!)

Well, God's people during this time of Jacob's trouble are very familiar with their sins. That's because they have a clear understanding of their past life and actions, and they see little good in *any* of it! And so they're remorseful. They have accepted God's peace that comes from His justifying grace (spoken of in Romans 5), and they know what it means to receive pardon. But, they still have remorse for having done what they did in certain circumstances—and having let God down. So, they're struggling with this and feeling hopeless and helpless. (By the way, none of these modern "perfectionists" will be among them—these people who hang around God's people saying they haven't sinned for five years.)

Preserving God's Name

But their *biggest* concern, the one that troubles them the most, goes much deeper than worry about their own skin. I'd like to shout it from the housetops today, because it's a point many have missed.

Though God's people will be surrounded by enemies bent on their destruction, the anguish and pain which they suffer is not the dread of persecution. If they could be assured of pardon, they would not shrink from torture or from death. But their suffering is based on this: that if they prove unworthy and lose their lives because of their own character defects, then *God's holy name* would be brought under reproach. Their concern is not for themselves, but for God! They long for, once again, the assurance of God's pardon, His justifying grace, because they don't want to see God hurt.

After he failed at the rock in the wilderness (and struck it, instead of speaking to it), Moses asked God's forgiveness and God forgave him—but he carried the remorse of that failure later as he climbed Mount Nebo to his death. It must have been heavy on his mind, as he once again accepted the righteousness of Christ instead of his own failures. Even as Moses prepared to fall asleep in God's arms, there was still remorse for having brought God's name into ill repute.

People who struggle by their own Brook Jabbok are not struggling because they're afraid they're not going to make it to the Heavenly country. And they're not struggling because they're afraid that they may have forgotten one sin. They're struggling because they don't want God's name to come into ill repute.

And this is a pattern that they have developed earlier, not just at the spur of the moment. People who are really God's people are more concerned with God's reputation than they are their own fate. Moses had proved that long ago when he said, "Blot out my name, if that's what it takes. But don't let your name come into ill repute."

God's Assurance

So, what's the *solution* to the stress that these people go through as they wrestle by their own Brook Jabbok during this time of trouble?

First of all, they can have the assurance of pardon. Had not Jacob previously repented of his sin in obtaining the birthright by fraud, God would not have heard his prayer and mercifully preserved his life. If, during the time of trouble, God's people had unconfessed sins appear before them (while they were already tortured with fear and anguish), they would be overwhelmed—despair would cut off their faith, and they wouldn't have the confidence to plead with God for deliverance. But even though they have a deep sense of their own unworthiness, they have no concealed wrongs to reveal. Their sins have gone beforehand to judgment, and have been blotted out, and they can not bring them back into remembrance. So, can we have assurance during the time of Jacob's trouble? Yes!

And another factor that's quite obvious, if you study the sequence of events, is that these people wouldn't even *be* in this position if they weren't already on God's side. This is *after* the close of probation, when everybody who is righteous is righteous still and everyone who is unrighteous is unrighteous still. Nobody crosses the line during the time of Jacob's trouble.

I began to study this topic sort of teetering with an idea: Suppose I don't have that kind of faith, and I don't make it through the time of Jacob's trouble—what will I do? Will I curse God and die? Will I join the ranks of the enemy? No, that's not the scenario at all. *No one* crosses the line at this time. If we find ourselves in the time of Jacob's trouble, we're there to the finish. Or, to put it another way, if we make it *to* the time of Jacob's trouble, we'll make it *through* the time of Jacob's trouble. No one will check out, regardless of the stress.

Another part of the solution is the friendly voice of God, who says, "*I* will not let *you* go, until I bless you." And like Jacob of old, he gives us a new name. (A new name? Great! I've always hated my name, so I'm looking forward to that!) A new name carries spiritual significance and meaning with it. Jacob was no longer a cheat and a liar; now he was, by name, a prince of God. And we also have the assurance, as God's people, that we're going in to possess the land of our fathers—that beautiful land especially designed for happiness.

Preserving God's Name

Will there be stress? Yes. Will people wrestle in anguish? Yes. (But isn't it good to know this ahead of time, so it doesn't surprise us?) But part of our anguish will come from failing to distinguish between faith and feeling.

Not long ago we visited the Rocky Mountain "Outward Bound" school, and took a look at the stringent obstacle course the young people follow as they try to become great mountain people. As I stood there, looking up, something came over me, and foolishly I wanted to give it a try. So I started climbing the rope ladders that led up into the treetops. Then, I discovered, you have to swing from here to there, and from there to the other place! And then you walk across teetering planks, barely wide enough to hook your fingernails into. Finally, at the end of the course (about halfway to the stars), you're supposed to bail out into a net about ten thousand feet below! Now I'd seen some of those outward bound people doing it already. And I knew it was all right. But I just didn't *feel* like doing it.

When God's people come to the time of Jacob's trouble, they will have seen what's gone before, and they'll know that it's all right. But it won't *feel* good! And in that day we'll have to understand the difference between faith and feeling.

No Turning Back

Some people enjoy bunjee jumping. I met a pastor's wife who doesn't get her thrills from shopping—she goes bunjee jumping! "Wow!" I said to the pastor, "Do you do that?" "No," he said, "I'm the one who *drives* her to it." They tell me that people pay up to sixty dollars to do this. Sometimes timid people go up—and they sit there forever. They try to go off slowly. They try to slide off. They stand back up and try to jump off. But they can't jump! Finally they creep back down and hope to get their sixty dollars back.

But the time of Jacob's trouble is not like that. No, you don't back down at this point. If you're one of God's people *before* this happens, you'll be one of God's people through it all. There will be times (because extreme stress has been predicted) when your feelings will get pretty jangled.

But through everything, we'll know that it's all right. And the One who has promised to see us through, will stay right beside us.

"We are climbing Jacob's ladder.
We are climbing Jacob's ladder.
We are climbing Jacob's ladder.
Soldiers of the cross.

Every round goes higher, higher.
Every round goes higher, higher.
Every round goes higher, higher.
Soldiers of the cross.

Sinner, do you love my Jesus?
Sinner, do you love my Jesus?
Sinner, do you love my Jesus?
Soldiers of the cross.

If you love Him, why not serve Him?
If you love Him, why not serve Him?
If you love Him, why not serve Him?
Soldiers of the cross."[1]

[1] American Negro Spiritual

Chapter Sixteen

Without an INTERCESSOR

How many of you are into vacuum cleaners? I've been around vacuum cleaners most of my life. It goes back to childhood when one of my duties, on Friday afternoon, was vacuuming. This included taking off the regular attachments, putting on the upholstery parts, doing all the furniture—everything. When my mother wasn't looking, I'd sometimes play around a little bit; try sucking my cheeks out and things like that. I tried vacuuming my eyebrows one time. That wasn't too smart. And I turned it on my hair once, not knowing then that I'd live to regret that!

But one thing was pretty clear. When you go down the hall and try to do one more room (still plugged into the same socket) and the plug pulls loose, you're in trouble. You've got to be connected to the power source if you're going to get anywhere.

Now you could go push the plug in, and then try to make the thing work better by turning it upside down and pushing on the roller brushes. But that would be foolish. It's an insult to the power source if you think you have to do something *in addition* to plugging in.

When we talk about vacuum cleaners (or San Francisco trolleys, or "the vine and the branches"), we know we're not going anywhere unless we're connected to the source of power. Which leads us to a myth and misunderstanding that's been around a long time. It's this: "There's a point during the end time of trouble when you have to be on your own power." Have you ever heard this? It's called "being without an intercessor." Some people have gotten the idea that we're going to need enough "righteousness by battery storage" or "righteousness by habit" to *coast* through this time when we'll be out of contact with the power source.

This is gross deception! In the first place, it isn't true. And in the second, it can lead to real discouragement for weak people—and big surprises for the strong!

Let's talk about this misconception. First, I'd like to look at it from the standpoint of an answer I tried to give yesteryear. Then, I'd like to present a "new" thought about living without an intercessor. (Have you ever had your brain "split open" from a brand-new idea? It's exhilarating—especially when the idea is so obvious you suddenly realize how dense you've been!)

Dependence and Intercession

First, I'd like to take the position (without even trying to prove it at the moment), that no created being of God, whether born sinner or unfallen angel, ever lives on their own power. It's impossible. We have no power for life. In spite of our genius and advanced science, mankind hasn't even come close to creating life. So, we're dependent on God for life, for every beat of our hearts.

We're also dependent upon God for righteousness. We know from Scripture (and from hard personal experience—the bumps and bruises of trying) that all our attempts at righteousness are only going to end up as filthy rags. So, *dependence* is a key concept for life and righteousness with every being that God has ever created.

And that just doesn't fit with the idea that sometime in the future we'll be running on our own steam.

Let's take a closer, Scriptural look at this concept of an intercessor. Isaiah 53 contains the famous chapter on the suffering Christ—the one that says He was pierced for our transgressions and crushed for our iniquities. "He poured out his life unto death..." (This is your Savior, we're talking about.) "...and was numbered with the transgressors..." (That's good news for transgressors.) "For he bore the sin of many and *made intercession* for the transgressors." (Isaiah 53:12) And so Jesus our Lord, because of His death and what followed, is an intercessor for the transgressors.

Here's a text (Romans 8:26) that includes another member of the Godhead, the Holy Spirit. "In the same way, the Spirit helps us in our weakness. We do not know what we ought to pray..." (We don't even know how to pray right! I'm glad God allows us to acknowledge that.) "...but the Spirit himself intercedes for us with groans that words cannot express." This text clearly indicates that the Holy Spirit is also an intercessor, or "go-between"; someone who *intervenes* when we have a problem.

(By the way, some people interpret this text to support speaking in unknown tongues. But it's not referring to *us*—it's talking about the *Holy Spirit's* power to intercede for us.)

Now, we come to a very significant text in this discussion. It says, "Therefore he [Jesus] is able to save completely those who come to God through him..." (Do *you* need to be saved *completely*, or do you figure you're just sort of a halfway sinner? The more we come to Jesus, the more we realize His presence, and the more we know that we *all* need to be saved to the uttermost! I've seen people carrying Oswald Chambers' My Utmost for His Highest. It's a good example of this. We're grateful to the utmost for Jesus saving to the uttermost.) The text continues, "...because He always lives to intercede for them." (Hebrews 7:25).

How long will He intercede? Does this text mean "He lives to intercede until the close of probation"? No way! It says He's *always* there to intervene for us.

So away with this idea that a time will come when we'll have no intercessor. Of course, this leads to the question, "How did some people come up with this idea they must live without an intercessor?"

Promise of His Presence

Before we answer that, let's bring in one more assurance from Scripture that God doesn't plan to abandon us to our own resources. Even though he doesn't use the word "intercessor," the Apostle Paul sums it up nicely in Romans 8:38,39. "For I am convinced that neither death nor life, neither angels nor demons, neither the present nor the future, nor any powers, neither height nor depth, nor anything else in all creation, will be able to separate us from the love of God that is in Christ Jesus our Lord." Paul pulls out all the stops to remind us that nothing can separate us from Jesus (except ourselves). Jesus still stands by His original promise, "Lo, I am with you always..." Even until the close of probation? No, "...even until the end of the world"! That at least takes us past the close of probation. And, the last time I checked, the end of the world is only the beginning of forever, where He'll continue "ever living to make intercession for us." Whether He's inside the heavenly sanctuary or not? Yes!

Let's also look back at Daniel 12:1, the text that leads into the close of probation and the time of trouble such as never was. "At that time Michael [Christ], the great prince who protects your people, will arise." (Protects whose people? Daniel's. And who was Daniel? One of the Jews, God's chosen people at that time. And what's the modern application? Galatians 3:29—"If you belong to Christ, then you are Abraham's seed, and heirs according to the promise.") So here we have Christ standing up for you and for me at the close of probation. He's not abandoning us. He's standing up for us—like the day Stephen was being stoned, and he looked up into heaven and saw Jesus standing beside the Father. When trouble comes upon His people, Jesus doesn't take it sitting down! He stands up for us. Does that sound like we're abandoned, left on our own? No way! The reality is that Jesus continuously intercedes for our salvation.

Notice the key thought, the qualifying word here. We will never be without an intercessor for our *salvation.* So, if we're ever "without an intercessor," it must be for something else. And this is the thought that's brand-new for many of us. We'll discuss it in a moment.

The Work of Intercession

In the meantime, let's look at what being an "intercessor" is all about. Christ is the high priest of the church and He has a work to perform which no one else can do. By His grace, He's able to keep His creatures from transgression—that's part of His work in heaven. Angels, unfallen worlds, and saints who've accepted His grace are included in His intercessory work.

It's as necessary for Christ to *keep* us by His intercession as it is for Him to *redeem* us through His blood. His power to keep us from falling is just as necessary as His forgiveness. Those purchased by His blood, He now keeps by His intercession. Can you see the connection here? The two aspects of Christ's righteousness are *pardon* and *power*. (Want to get theological? Call them justification and sanctification.) Both are involved in His intercessory work.

Christ constantly mediates in behalf of man. (The words mediator and intercessor are rather synonymous.) And His work as mediator, or intercessor, is what keeps other worlds from sin—worlds that have discovered they can only keep from falling by relying on His constant power. Adam, to our dismay, discovered what happens when man tries to live without God's constant power. Let's admit it—we *need* Him. We're not even big enough to keep our own hearts beating, let alone live righteously. So, when we talk about "intercession," we must include the concepts of pardon and power.

A Popular Explanation

One popular concept of "living without an intercessor" goes like this: Those who are alive when Jesus comes will have discovered how to let God lead them. They totally accept His power, which then keeps them from falling anymore. That puts the heavenly ministry out of business, because it's no longer needed for the pardon of sins. So the idea is that there will be a group of people who overcome because they now totally understand Christ's intercession *power,* as well as His pardon. And when you're not sinning anymore (because you are accepting His power), you don't *need* His pardon.

But wait a minute. Don't you still need intercession for the past, as well as for present power? And there are other problems with this concept, too. A big one is that people then become preoccupied with becoming "perfect." And we don't need *that* kind of inward focus!

The idea of Jesus leaving the heavenly sanctuary (and not needing to forgive us anymore) leads to yet another problem. It has to do with why we need His justifying grace and His forgiveness in the first place. Intercession involves more than just our present sinning. We all have a bad track record, don't we? And, even if we live perfectly for a million years, it won't change our past. Why can God take our track record and cast it into the depths of the sea and remember it no more? Because of Christ's intercessory work in terms of forgiveness. His justifying grace continues to take care of our past—forever.

Therefore, even if I never sin again from this moment on, I still need His intercession (in terms of pardon), because of my past! We'd better be very careful about doing away with Christ's intercession for pardon, because this carries with it big problems.

No Need for Intercession?

In an attempt to explain "without an intercessor" in an earlier book,

I wrote something quite similar to what I just described. "God will have brought us by His grace to a point where we will no longer need an Intercessor for forgiveness of sins, since we will have been given the victory. But we will always and forever need His intercession for keeping power. In fact, the reason we will no longer need His intercession for sinning is that we will have discovered His intercession for keeping power." Well, it sounded pretty good at the time, and I was convinced.

But what about those who come to Christ thirty minutes before probation closes? They haven't had a lifetime to be transformed by grace and become overcomers. Won't they need forgiveness during the time of trouble? Is it possible that one of them might lose his patience and at least *want* to punch out some arrogant, right-wing, moral majority type—and then need forgiveness?

And what about the thief on the cross? He surely didn't have time to grow. Do we open the door for some kind of painless, supernatural surgery on the righteous dead (who haven't completed the job), *and* on those who boarded the last trolley just before it left? There's a problem here!

(Now I'm not suggesting that sinning will continue in heaven. I don't believe that. Three problems that give us so much trouble—the world, the flesh, and the devil—will be gone when heaven comes. Besides, we'll be so enthralled with constant dependence on a loving, visible God that no one will choose to separate again—forever.)

Four Groups

Here's an interesting concept that relates to this dilemma. Look at Revelation 22:11. (KJV) Probation is closing, and Michael stands up. "He that is unjust, let him be unjust still: and he which is filthy, let him be filthy still: and he that is righteous, let him be righteous still: and he that is holy, let him be holy still."

Now it had never even crossed my mind before—why did God list *four* groups of people? He could have simply said, "He that's righteous, stay righteous; he that's unrighteous, stay unrighteous." But instead, we have these four groups. So, who could they be?

Well, the first one is obvious: "He that is unjust, let him be unjust still." That's the person who never did accept God's justifying grace and who persisted to the end in resisting the pleadings of the Holy Spirit. This person never was a Christian and never intended to be.

Then "He that is filthy, let him be filthy still." That's an interesting one. We'll come back to that in a moment.

"He that is righteous, let him be righteous still." Who's that? That's the thief on the cross who died shortly after he accepted Christ. Was he righteous? Yes, because of Jesus. This group could include those who accept Christ moments before the close of probation. Righteous? Yes—covered by Christ's imputed righteousness.

"And he that is holy, let him be holy still." Could this be the one hundred and forty-four thousand? Are these people the ones who've been on the way, who've grown, and who've learned both aspects of Christ's intercession—both pardon and power? This group would be the overcomers, the ones not sinning anymore. (And don't think that's impossible. Scripture makes it clear that there is overcoming power available before Jesus comes.)

Now looking at these groups, perhaps the "filthy" one becomes clear just by the process of elimination. I punched "filthy" into my computer (you know, all the "filthies" in the Bible), and there aren't that many. But it appears this group has something to do with people who've been trying to produce their own righteousness. All they can come up with is rags, filthy rags. (And they're going to remain that way unless they accept something better before this time.) Perhaps filthy could also include those who once accepted, but turned away and slid back into the mud—backsliders.

Anyway, there must be some reason why God indicated four groups here, groups that are now set in cement as probation closes. Could it be possible that there will be a group who won't need God's forgiveness for continued sinning before Jesus comes? Yes. Will they still need His justifying grace for their past? Yes. Can they get along without an intercessor for power? No way! Can anyone get along without an intercessor—angels, unfallen worlds, or saints? No, it's impossible to go through *any* time without Christ's intercession for salvation from falling. So, when that time comes, in what sense will our world be "without an intercessor"?

Without Intercession

Here's where I began to feel rather foolish, because the answer was so obvious. (Why don't we just read with our eyes open, instead of remembering what we've *heard* all our lives? We need to be like the Bereans and check it out to "see whether these things be so".)

Let me use a modern illustration. Not long ago, a maniac in the Middle East was responsible for the death of thousands and thousands of people. Then someone came along and "interceded"—Bush, Powell, Schwarzkopf, and company. They *intervened*. The United States took the lead, and interceded in a tough situation. Otherwise, many believe, it would have been much, much worse. Anyway, this illustration can help us understand how we'll be without an intercessor when Christ throws down the censor.

When Christ leaves the sanctuary in heaven, darkness will cover the inhabitants of the earth. In that fearful time the righteous must live in the sight of a Holy God "without an intercessor." *The restraint which has been upon the wicked is now removed and Satan has entire control.* God's long-suffering (His intercession, if you will) has ended. The world has rejected His grace, despised His mercy, and trampled upon His law. The wicked have passed the boundary of probation. *The Spirit of God,* persistently resisted, *has at last been withdrawn.* Unsheltered by Divine grace, they (the wicked) have no protection from the wicked one. Satan will then plunge the inhabitants of the earth into one great final trouble. As the angels of God cease to hold back the fierce winds of human passion, all the elements of strife will be let loose. The whole world will be involved in ruin more terrible than that which came upon Jerusalem of old. The same destructive power exercised by holy angels at God's command will be exercised by evil angels when God's Spirit withdraws from the wicked.

So what's the intercession we're talking about here? It's God's intervening power that has kept this world from falling apart. And now it is withdrawn, it's gone. When there is no longer an intercessor against Satan, and God's angels release those four winds, then "all hell breaks loose."

That's what it means. Both the righteous and the wicked will live without an intercessor against global ruin. Scary? Yes! Will *we* be scared? Well, probably so—we're still human and we still have feelings. It will be a scary time. But we don't need to be *afraid* of this time. If you are one of God's people, then you'll probably be in one of three places during this time: You'll either be in prison (don't let that frighten you because the angels can make a prison a palace), or you'll be fleeing toward the mountains and the rocks, or you'll have already arrived there and be hiding.

And don't forget, there are some mighty promises for God's people wherever they are during this time. Your bread and water will be sure (although not the ice cream or cake). And, you'll have the forces of heaven doubled, and tripled, and quadrupled around you—because the angels who've left the wicked (and the Holy Spirit who has left the wicked because they wouldn't have Him), have now completely surrounded God's people.

Alone? Never! On our own power? Never! God's love for His children during the period of their severest trial is as strong and as tender as in the days of their sunniest prosperity. But they must endure the fires of affliction, so that their earthliness is consumed, and they perfectly reflect the image of Christ. Evidently God has a purpose for the stress His people will go through. And, perhaps, that's how some who come to Christ moments before the close of probation can grow as much in this short time as others have in years.

Pardon and Power Forever

Well, what can we gain from these insights? I, for one, am thankful to get it straight in my own heart that Christ's intercession and mediation in my behalf (for both pardon and power) will continue unbroken forever. And the only thing that really counts at this point is that the Lord is coming—are you ready?

If you've been a victim of the idea (picked up at home, or school, or church, or wherever) that in order to *get* ready and to *be* ready, you've got to start *trying harder* to live a better life—then forget it. *Forget it!* There's only *one thing* we can ever do to prepare, and that's get our "vacuum cleaners plugged in"; our "trolley reconnected to the power above"; our "branches reunited with the Vine."

And how do you do that? It's so simple that any child can understand it. You go to your knees (as you read your Bible, and study the life of Christ) and daily seek to understand Him better as your very best friend. That's it!

And, if I don't have time to do that, then I really don't have time to live, not even for another moment—because that's the way I accept Christ's intercessory work in my behalf.

Those who delay preparing for the day of God *cannot* obtain it in the times of trouble—or at any subsequent time. The case of all such procrastinators is hopeless.

We *must* take time from our "busy" schedules to pray and reflect on Him. If we allow our minds to be absorbed (or even distracted) by the world, then God may give us time to think by removing whatever idols stand in our way—be they gold, or houses, or even T.V.! Why? Because He loves us! Why not admit that you need Him today?

Here's a song of confession and admission. And if you find yourself in the picture, then sing these words in your heart, right now.

"I need Thee, precious Jesus, for I am very poor;
A stranger and a pilgrim, I have no earthly store.
I need the love of Jesus to cheer me on my way,
To guide my doubting footsteps, to be my strength and stay.

I need Thee, precious Jesus. I hope to see Thee soon,
Encircled with the rainbow, and seated on Thy throne.
There, with Thy blood-bought children, my joy shall ever be
To sing Thy ceaseless praises. To gaze, my Lord, on Thee!"[1]

[1] Frederick Whitefield

Chapter Seventeen

God's People DELIVERED

The other morning I was walking the mile or so from my house to my office. A carload of guys came by. They slowed down and opened the windows. Then they hung their heads out and cussed at me! They yelled obscenities! And the only thing that I'd done to deserve this was getting born.

I began to think about it. Why was that the best they could do to start my morning (which is ordinarily a beautiful time of day)? Last I checked, people like that still have the Holy Spirit and the angels working on them. But, one of these days, we're going to be faced with a time when the Holy Spirit and the angels have withdrawn from everyone who's not interested—and all hell will break loose.

Of course, the one big comfort is that all heaven will break loose as well. And now we're coming to the most exciting part of this book on last day events—the time when Jesus comes! Finally we're going to explore that time period when God *delivers* His people from all the stress, all the bumps and bruises of planet earth.

I want to share with you a graphic picture of God's people being delivered from a world of sin. Let's set the stage for this description by reading from the sixteenth chapter of Revelation, where the sixth and seventh plagues are breaking out.

"The seventh angel poured out his bowl into the air, and out of the temple came a loud voice from the throne, saying, 'It is done!' Then there came flashes of lightning, rumblings, peals of thunder, and a severe earthquake. No earthquake like it has ever occurred since man has been on earth, so tremendous was the quake...Every island fled away and the mountains could not be found. From the sky huge hailstones of about a hundred pounds each fell upon men. And they cursed God on account of the plague of hail, because the plague was so terrible." (Revelation 16:17-20).

What a combination! When you're in an earthquake you want to run outside—but when you're in a hailstorm you want to run inside! So there's *no* place to hide!

The Two Groups

As we begin to look at the world-shaking events that will occur during this time, let's quickly review the path that these two groups (righteous and unrighteous) have been traveling.

First of all, there's been a big shakeup during "the shaking time." Personally, I believe it started in the late 1950's and has been going on ever since. And it's becoming more intense every day. The righteous are shaken in and the unrighteous are shaken out.

There's also a true revival that takes place among God's people. This includes the latter rain, the loud cry, and the Holy Spirit.

At the same time there's a false revival, complete with Satan's delusions among the unrighteous.

Among God's people, total dependence upon God develops; among the unrighteous, total dependence upon self.

Both groups experience global crises, probably in at least three major areas: economic, nuclear, and natural disasters.

Also during this time, a group of people (the righteous) experience the seal of God—represented by God's day of worship since creation, and the unrighteous experience "the mark of the beast"—represented by the false day of worship set up by man.

Finally, persecution arises, the church is sifted, and only those who are serious stay in. (And among the unrighteous there are plenty of persecutors and sifters that are happy to do the job.)

The Main Events

We've also noticed that there's a time without intercession after the close of probation. We've found that "without an intercessor" doesn't mean Jesus will abandon us (in terms of our spiritual needs and resources)—it simply means that heaven will no longer intervene to prevent world ruin. God Himself commands the four winds to be released and everything breaks loose.

Also, during this great time of trouble, the seven last plagues will occur. God's people are saved from them, but the unrighteous are not.

Then we have the false second coming of Christ put on by Satan; an apparently spectacular event staged under the sixth plague. The devil takes over as world leader, and convinces everyone that the reason for all the trouble is because the opposition (God's people) are not in his camp.

And there's the "time of Jacob's trouble." Here God's people experience tremendous stress and turmoil, even discouragement.

Following these things (under the seventh plague) God steps in to deliver His people. Panic fills the unrighteous as they see what's happening, and realize they've been on the wrong side.

Then comes the special resurrection. This is the time when many sleeping saints awake to life eternal. But at the same time, the world is bathed in blood, because the unrighteous (or wicked) are so ugly and filled with hate, they begin to kill *each other!*

There you have it—the path of the righteous and the unrighteous. On one hand, life; on the other hand, death.

And It Shall Come to Pass...

Now share with me this graphic picture, and let your imagination flow as we envision the scene:

The time predicted approaches. Soon those who honor God will no longer be protected by human laws. In various nations around the globe, plans are being made to bring about their destruction. God's people will be given one last chance to recant. The ultimatum—join us or die! When the time arrives, the wicked plan to strike a final, decisive blow; one to silence the voices of reproof forever.

The deadline nears. God's people (some in prison cells, others hidden in isolated parts of the mountains and forests) plead for divine protection. On every side, companies of armed men, urged on by hosts of evil angels, prepare for this work of death and destruction.

Finally the moment arrives. With coarse jeering and shouts of triumph, throngs of evil men rush toward their prey. Suddenly a dense blackness, deeper than the darkness of night, falls on the earth. A rainbow, shining with the glory of God, spans the heavens. It seems to encircle each praying company. The angry multitudes freeze; their mocking cries die on the wind. With fearful eyes, they gaze on this symbol of God's covenant. Its brightness overpowers them.

Then God's people hear a clear, melodious voice calling, "Look up." The black, angry clouds roll back, and the righteous lift their eyes (like Stephen of old) to see the glory of God with Jesus standing by the throne. They see the nailprints in His hands, the scars on His brow. And from His own lips, in the presence of His Father and the holy angels, they hear Him proclaim, "I would like these people, the ones You have given Me, to come and be with Me now."

Again His voice, musical and triumphant, is heard saying, "And now they come! They come! Holy, harmless, and undefiled. They have kept My word; they shall walk among the angels!" And the pale, quivering lips of those who have held fast to their faith break forth with a mighty shout of victory.

It is at midnight when God displays His awesome power to deliver His people. Suddenly the sun bursts forth, shining in strength. Other signs and wonders follow in quick succession. Nature seems to be turned upside down. Streams cease to flow. Dark, ominous clouds crash together. The wicked look about in amazement and terror, but the righteous greet these tokens of deliverance with unspeakable joy.

In the very center of the angry heavens there appears a clear space of indescribable glory. Out of it comes the voice of God, like an enormous waterfall, thundering, "It is done." The power of His voice rocks the heavens and the earth.

A global earthquake begins with destruction far surpassing any ever known by man. The sky appears to rip open, then slam shut again. Glorious beams of brilliant light flash from the throne of God. Mountains sway like grass in winter wind, huge boulders plunge down their ragged sides. Lashed into fury, the sea produces enormous waves that crush everything in their path. The shriek of a thousand hurricanes fills the air—like the voice of demons bent on destruction. The earth heaves and swells, it's surface crumbles. Its very foundations seem to give way. Mountain chains sink, islands disappear, entire seaports are swallowed up by angry waters.

And then huge hailstones begin to fall. These enormous projectiles (weighing up to 100 pounds each) continue the mass destruction. Proud cities are smashed into ruins. Lordly palaces, where great men lavished their wealth in self-glory, are beaten to pieces before their eyes. Prison walls burst open and God's people (held in bondage for their faith) go free.

Graves begin to open. "Multitudes who sleep in the dust of the earth will awake: some to everlasting life, others to shame and everlasting contempt." (Daniel 12:2—the special resurrection.) Those who have died with faith in Jesus, who stood for truth in the last days, come forth glorified to hear God declare His covenant of peace with those who have kept His law. "They also which pierced Him"—those who mocked Christ's dying agonies (and the most violent opposers of

His truth and His people) are raised to behold Him in His glory and to see the honor placed on the loyal and obedient.

Those who sacrificed all for Christ are now secure. They have been tested before the world, before the despisers of truth, and have demonstrated their trusting obedience in Him. Faced with dark and terrible deaths, they've stood firm for the One who died for them.

Now, miraculously delivered from evil men and demonic spirits, a marvelous change suddenly transforms them. Faces that moments before were pale, anxious, and haggard are now aglow with wonder, faith, and love. Triumphantly they begin to sing, "God is our refuge and strength, an everpresent help in trouble. Therefore we will not fear, though the earth give way and the mountains fall into the heart of the sea, though its waters roar and foam and the mountains quake with their surging."

As these words of holy trust ascend to God, the clouds roll back to reveal the starry heavens, unspeakably glorious in contrast with the angry clouds on either side. A mighty hand appears holding two tables of stone. As God's ten eternal principles (brief, comprehensive, and authoritative) are once again presented to the inhabitants of the earth, memory is stirred and conscience awakened.

God's people stand firm, their eyes fixed upward, their faces aglow with His glory (like the face of Moses as he came down from Sinai). And the wicked cannot bear to look upon them.

Soon a small dark cloud appears in the east. At first it seems smaller than a man's hand—but God's people recognize this sign. Even though distance shrouds it in darkness, they know that this cloud holds their Savior. They watch in solemn silence as it draws nearer, becoming brighter and more glorious every moment. Now from this immense, snow-white cloud, Jesus rides forth as a mighty conqueror. No longer a "Man of Sorrow" to drink the bitter cup of shame and woe, now He comes as the victor of heaven and earth.

With anthems of celestial melody, a vast throng of holy angels attend Him on His way. The sky is bursting with radiant forms—"ten thousand times ten thousand, and thousands of thousands."

As the living cloud comes closer, every eye beholds the King. No crown of thorns now mars His sacred head, a crown of glory rests on that holy brow. His dazzling countenance outshines the sun. Before His presence *all* faces pale, and those who rejected God's mercy feel the terror of eternal despair. Trembling, even the righteous cry, "Who shall be able to stand?" The angels' song is hushed and there is a moment of awful silence. Then Jesus says to them, "My grace is sufficient for you"—and joy fills the hearts of the righteous.

Now the angels strike a higher note and draw still nearer the earth. The King of kings descends on His cloud. The heavens roll together as a scroll, and the earth trembles before Him. Derisive jests have long since ceased, lying lips are hushed in silence. The only human sounds are voices raised in prayer, or in weeping and despair. The wicked cry for the rocks to bury them. They cannot face the One they've despised and rejected. How often that Voice (in the tender loving tones of a friend, a brother, a Redeemer) has entreated them to repentance. Now painful memories awake—the warnings despised, the invitations refused, the privileges slighted.

Those who mocked Christ in His humiliation and derided His claim to be the Son of God now behold Him in His glory. Haughty Herod who jeered at His royal title, the mocking soldiers who crowned Him with thorns, wicked men who smote and spat upon the Prince of life—all seek to flee from His overpowering glory. Those who drove the nails through His hands and feet, who pierced His side, behold these marks with terror and remorse. With shuddering horror, priests and rulers remember how they taunted Him saying, "He saved others but he can't save himself!...Let him come down now from the cross, and we will believe in him. He trusts in God. Let God rescue him now if He wants him!"

Those who would have destroyed Christ and His faithful people now witness the glory that rests upon them. Consumed with terror they hear the saints joyfully singing, "Surely this is our God! We trusted him, and he saved us!" (Isaiah 25:9)

Now, as the earth reels and the lightning flashes, the voice of Jesus calls forth the sleeping saints. Looking on the graves of the righteous dead, He raises His hands to heaven, and cries, "Awake, awake, awake! You that sleep in the dust, arise!" Throughout the length and breadth of the earth, the dead hear His voice. From the prison of death they come, clothed with immortal glory, singing, "Where, O death, is your victory? Where, O death is your sting?" (1 Corinthians 15:55)

And the living righteous join the risen saints as their voices unite in a long, glad shout of victory. The living righteous are changed "in a moment, in the twinkling of an eye", and with the risen saints are caught up to meet the Lord in the air. Angels quickly gather His elect from the four winds, from one end of the earth to the other. Little children are borne by holy angels to their mothers' arms. Friends long separated by death are reunited, nevermore to part. And with songs of gladness, the righteous begin ascending to the City of God.

Oh wonderful moment of redemption—long talked of, long hoped for, long contemplated with eager anticipation (but never fully understood)—it has come at last!

"We have this hope that burns within our hearts,
Hope in the coming of the Lord.
We have this faith that Christ alone imparts,
Faith in the promise of His Word.
We believe the time is here,
When the nations far and near
Shall awake, and shout, and sing
Hallelujah! Christ is King!
We have this hope that burns within our hearts,
Hope in the coming of our Lord."[1]

[1] Wayne Hooper

Chapter Eighteen

Adam Meets ADAM

Not long before my mother passed away, my brother made the mistake of telling her that he planned to be cremated when he died. Wow! Her reaction was worse than when we were kids and we raided the candy dish between meals! She figuratively did a couple of "two and a half gainers," ran clear around the house three or four times, and almost had a coronary on the spot. She made him promise, right then, that he wouldn't *do* that! (So, I'm the only one who has a choice left now.)

Whether you're pro-ashes, or pro-dust, (or even in favor of not dying at all before Jesus comes) the important thing is that we stand firm in the promise of His coming. Long ago, the Apostle Peter warned us that, "...in the last days scoffers will come, scoffing and following their own evil desires. They will say, 'Where is this 'coming' he promised? Ever since our fathers died, everything goes on as it has since the beginning...'" (2 Peter 3:3,4)

Did you know there are at least eight times as many texts in your Bible on the *second* coming of Christ as there are on His first ? Many of these texts are very familiar to all of us "adventists" (whether you're a Methodist, a Baptist, or a Catholic —any one of us who believes in Christ's second advent is an "adventist"). And you could probably recite the major ones, like John 14:1-3, from memory. But I'd like to focus on a couple of the lesser known texts—including one that came from Jesus' own lips under oath.

Advent Promises

Jesus had been standing silently before his accusers and the whole Sanhedrin (a kangaroo court if ever there was one). Finally, frustrated at Christ's continued silence, the high priest shouted at him, "I charge you under oath by the living God: Tell us if you are the Christ, the Son of God." And Christ quietly replied, "It is as you say"—in other words, "You're right." And He could have ended it there, but He added something else (thus setting the stage for that special resurrection we talked about earlier). "But I say to all of you: In the future you will see the Son of Man sitting at the right hand of the Mighty One and coming on the clouds of heaven." (Matthew 26:64).

Jesus, under oath, promised He would return—because Jesus is in the habit of finishing what He starts! And He *will* finish the plan of salvation, for the plan has been in operation in the mind of God since before the foundation of the world.

Here's another advent text that may not be as familiar. "For the grace of God that brings salvation has appeared to all men..." (Sometimes we get the delusion that we're the only ones sharing God's grace with others. Paul reminds us that God's grace appears to *all* men. I'm glad there are bigger forces than you and I involved in this!) "...The grace of God...teaches us to say, 'No' to ungodliness and worldly passions, and to live self-controlled, upright, and godly lives in this present age, while we wait for the blessed hope—the glorious appearing of our great God and Savior, Jesus Christ..." (Titus 2:11-13)

Some of us used to think that the Father would remain in heaven, "keeping house" so to speak, while the Son came to fetch His friends.

But Paul implies that both God the Father *and* the Son are on this mission. And he calls this "glorious appearing" the "blessed hope".

1 Corinthians 15:19-22 is another common advent passage (with the familiar, "Behold, I show you a mystery")—but well-known as it is, perhaps there are additional insights we've missed. I've heard people say, "I think the Christian life is so wonderful, the life-style so rewarding, that I'd choose to be a Christian even without the promise of heaven or eternal life." I suppose we know what they mean and we shouldn't fault it. But Paul questions this attitude. "If only for this life we have hope in Christ, we are to be pitied more than all men." He's trying to remind us of the bigger picture. "...But Christ has indeed been raised from the dead, the firstfruits of those who have fallen asleep. For since death came through a man, the resurrection of the dead comes also through a man. For as in Adam all die, so in Christ all will be made alive." Then he proceeds with this "in Adam and in Christ" motif for the rest of the chapter.

The Second Adam

Sometimes Christians have struggled with these verses. But it's true that we're all "in Adam." When he fell, we fell. We can fault it, we can get angry about it—we can even shake our fists at God and say, "It isn't fair that you made the whole human race suffer for one man's mistake." (And some have done just that, looking to excuse their own doubts.) But, wait a minute! The second half of this passage is just as significant as the first. "For as *in Adam* all die, even so *in Christ* all will be made alive." Christ is the second Adam! Are you unhappy with your father, the father of the human race? Well then, you have a *new* Father, a perfect one! Jesus is our Savior, our Lord, and our Friend. He has also been called our elder Brother. But, here, Jesus is our new Father. As in Adam all die, even so in Christ all shall be made alive. Even though we are "in Adam" and reap the results of his sin, we can choose to be "in Christ" and reap the results of His sacrifice. One man sinned and caused *heartache* for millions; another man died and caused *salvation* for those millions. The two balance each other out. That's the good news of the Gospel!

But these two Adams are going to meet again someday soon—and it will be a touching moment. Meanwhile let's not get all bent out of shape because we were born on the wrong planet.

Besides, the more the years roll by, the more most of us realize we wouldn't *really* choose to live life over. Think about it. If you were asked (at the close of your three-score and ten) if you'd choose to live it all over again *exactly as you lived it* (no changes, no adjustments), you'd probably say, "No, thanks!" But, we don't have to wallow in it and have a pity party. There's a better way to look at it.

Instead of looking at yourself and your trials and pain, look at those around you in the same boat—and begin to have compassion for them. When you do that your own problems diminish. And when that happens, we're able to take an even broader view, and begin to look around at the universe and into God's heart that broke when sin came (and Jesus' heart that broke on the cross, and at Gethsemane). We even begin to have compassion for our Maker and look forward to the day when He is satisfied with His finished work. That's the bigger view. Perhaps Adam got a glimpse of this.

Adam & Eve

Let's go back and take a closer look at our earthly parents. There's not a whole lot about Adam—only about thirty-four texts in the whole Bible that even refer to him. As for Eve, there are about half a dozen. That's it. Commenting on Adam and Eve, someone once said that "the problem in the garden wasn't the apple in the tree; it was the 'pair' on the ground." Maybe so.

Now, Scripture says Adam and Eve were made in God's image. Interesting. God didn't just imagine some new form, then create it. He made us as an actual, physical image of Himself! Does that mean God has two eyes, and a nose, and a mouth, and two legs, and two hands? Evidently! Mankind was created to resemble his Maker.

What else do we know about this first pair? Well, indications are that when Adam enters heaven, they're going to have to raise the basketball hoops a bit—like twelve to fifteen feet! And Eve came up to his shoulders, and was incredibly beautiful.

God planned for Adam and Eve to stay together. This way they could support each other and not be tempted to approach the tree where the test was. But God created people with the power of choice, and Eve left Adam's side. Shortly thereafter, that separation was compounded, and resulted in further separation from God.

Before sin, Adam and Eve were covered with a beautiful garment of light. (Most artists have failed to accurately portray this.) But when they sinned, it was like unplugging the battery. The light was gone—so they tried to cover themselves with fig leaves. (Later, God tried to help them with this dilemma.)

Also, even before the fall, God gave them a useful occupation. Adam and Eve were happy and busy—training flowers, tending the garden, interacting with the animals. The happiest people I've ever known are those who have something useful to do; the unhappiest are the ones who don't have anything to do.

Now Eve listened to the serpent, but Adam listened to Eve. Adam made a deliberate choice, whereas Eve was deceived. And His choice was based on the hope that taking a chance might just work.

A student at one of our American colleges asked a psychology professor, "Will it make any difference in a person's life if they fall into a sexual sin?" And the professor replied, "I don't know what difference one act could make. After all, what's fifteen minutes?" Well, fifteen minutes can make a *big* difference. In this case it made a difference for the whole human race. Adam made a conscious choice to take this risk with Eve. Some have said, "Adam shouldn't have done that because God could have made him another Eve". Well, I'm a little sympathetic with Adam—the *first* Eve is the one he loved! But the problem wasn't that He loved Eve. The problem was that he forgot to love and trust His Maker! And that was the fatal choice.

Count Your Blessings

So there was a separation from God. As they left the garden, they must have been torn apart, must have pleaded with God to let them stay. And from that moment, the earth began to go farther and farther downhill. Imagine the remorse Adam felt for the rest of his life—and not just the "three-score years and ten" that we're allotted. Adam lived nine hundred and thirty years! (Genesis 5:5).

Often we don't appreciate what we have until it's gone. You don't really appreciate water until you turn the tap and nothing comes out. Few of us are wise enough to consider our present blessings in the light of some day not having them. Those who learn this know what true happiness and gratitude are all about. Learn to appreciate your father and mother while they're still here; someday they'll be gone. Learn to appreciate your little ones while they're still around; someday they won't be. Our power of appreciation develops in proportion to carefully thinking through the blessings that we *might not have* someday—or painfully realizing, as did Adam and Eve, the blessings we had that are now gone.

The Garden of Eden was history. They couldn't enter it again. All around them they saw fallen leaves and fading flowers. They saw death and decay. And they saw blood flow as they killed the first lamb, representing the Messiah who was to come.

And they knew that future generations would point to them and say, "You're the cause of all of this pain, and heartache, and sorrow, and death." For over nine hundred years they had to live with this!

Can you imagine? Most of us can't take much more than our three score and ten!

So, for nine hundred and thirty years, Adam's heart continued to beat. I suppose the enemy beat him over the head unmercifully with guilt and remorse and the temptation to curse God and give up on the whole thing. (Maybe Eve did this. We never hear about her again.) Painful as it was, his life ended one day, and the obituary read: "Adam, father of mankind, dead at the age of 930."

Death and Resurrection

Now, what do we know about death and the resurrection? Well, according to Scripture, when we die we merely go to sleep. "The living know that they will die. But the dead know nothing." (Ecclesiastes 9:5) We're unconscious. There's no knowledge of the passing of time in the grave. So, the years *since* those nine hundred and thirty long years, will be only a short time for Adam. From the time he went to sleep, until the time of the resurrection, will seem like only a moment. I often think of this when I'm in a cemetery. Just a moment from now (to them) and they'll wake up again! As far as Adam is concerned, he's not in the grave any longer than someone who falls asleep fifteen minutes before Jesus comes.

"For the Lord himself will come down from heaven, with a loud command, with the voice of the archangel and with the trumpet call of God, and the dead in Christ will rise first. After that, we who are still alive and are left will be caught up with them in the clouds to meet the Lord in the air. And so we will be with the Lord forever." 1 Thessalonians 4:16,17. Evidently, God has in mind repopulating heaven with the saints from this earth. He had it in mind when Adam was created. He still has it in mind after sin and the fall. Think of the possibility that you, reading this book, will be one of those who repopulates heaven and takes the place of the fallen angels! Amazing!

What about this resurrection mystery—who can explain it? I can't. What happens to the ashes of Huss and Jerome that were thrown in the Rhine River and carried into the ocean? How about people whose ships went down at sea, and whose bodies were eaten by sharks and digested? How's God going to put all that back together again?

My father loved to read things about this. He came to me one day and shared one of his rare insights, one that settled it for him (in spite of my mother and my brother's discussion). "In the resurrection," he said, "God doesn't have to depend upon preexistent matter! Except for your loved one's emotions, it doesn't really matter what happens to your remains, because God has the master plan." In other words, God has your "program" in the master computer, and all He has to do is press the right button and you'll be back again—regardless of what happened to your body. A great mystery? Yes, of course. But it's no greater than the mystery of life.

Next time you look in the mirror, ask yourself, "What's keeping this thing going?" The only answer is God! We certainly don't keep our own hearts beating. (Although some people seem to chew gum fast enough to keep their heart beating—at least that's what my school teacher told us.) Yes, the wonder and mystery of life is as great as the wonder and mystery of the resurrection. You can't explain either one. And you can't produce them. Scientists and doctors have been able to take hearts out of chests and keep them beating, they've even been able to stop them and start them again. We can play around with life, analyze it, dissect it, and give it all kinds of classifications.

But we still can't *produce* life! It's *still* a wonder and a mystery, and will continue to be because God is the author of life—and who's big enough to understand that? That's why it says, "Behold I show you a *mystery*; we shall not all sleep, but we shall all be changed." And we know the resurrection (mysterious as it might be) is going to be *real*— just as real as the life you experience right now.

Among those who come forth in the resurrection will be father

Adam, and all the generations since him who have accepted God's great plan of salvation.

A Matter of Perspective

Now, what will be the effect of Jesus' coming on *you*? Well, that depends on your decision (and it's a continuing decision) concerning the Gospel.

In the days when Jesus was here the first time, He went into the temple and picked up a scourge of cords. He didn't use it on anyone (though they probably deserved it), but in His hand it looked like a mighty flaming sword. People threw their money to the four winds and fled from the temple in complete panic. But wait a minute! Not everyone ran away. Some were not frightened at all, including little children and widows, and the sick and maimed, and the halt and blind, and the humble and meek. As the others fled away, *they* pressed in closer and closer to Him.

So it all depends on your attitude toward Jesus, your attitude toward God. When Jesus comes back, we'll either be praying for the rocks and mountains to fall on us, or we'll be saying, "This is it! This is the One I've been waiting for!" It will make all the difference in the world "when Jesus comes to stay." Remember that old song?

> "One sat alone, beside the highway begging.
> His eyes were blind. The light he could not see.
> He clutched his rags and shivered in the shadows.
> Then Jesus came and bade his darkness flee.
>
> Unclean! Unclean! the leper cried in torment.
> The deaf, the dumb, in helplessness stood near.
> The fever raged, disease had gripped its victim.
> Then Jesus came, and cast out every fear.

When Jesus comes, the tempter's power is broken.
When Jesus comes, the tears are wiped away.
He takes the gloom and fills the life with glory,
For all is changed. When Jesus comes to stay."[1]

Mighty men will cry for the rocks and the mountains, while little children will push open the massive gates to the city of God. The righteous will throw away their glasses, and their canes, and their wheelchairs, and their hearing aids, and their heart valves. As my father used to say, "In the hereafter, in the glory country, we'll live with perfect bodies and perfect minds in a perfect world. And after we've lived a million years, we'll have just gotten started." (I'll go one better than my father—when we've lived a million years, we won't even have *begun* yet, because eternity has no beginning and no end!) "...and we'll never get tired, because the things that make us tired now will be gone. Gone forever!"

Everything Made New

When the trumpet sounds and the Lord descends, the resurrected righteous (and the living who have been caught up to meet Him in the air) begin a glorious week-long journey from earth to heaven. Will there be rest stops along the way? Campgrounds? Perhaps we'll be too busy exchanging experiences and reminiscing with united loved ones to need any breaks. We'll pass planets and suns and stars and entire solar systems, and finally come (perhaps through that long corridor in the open space of Orion) to heaven's gates.

But just before those gates open, there's going to be a touching moment everyone will see. Millions of people from every generation will be riveted to the scene. (I don't know how God lets everyone see, but He has His methods. After all, we understand about television, and satellites, and complex mass communications—and God *created* the physics principles underlying such things.)

[1] Oswald J. Smith

Picture it with me: As the ransomed ones are welcomed to the City of God, suddenly an exultant cry of adoration rings out. The two Adams are about to meet. The Son of God stands with outstretched arms to receive the father of our race—the one He created, the one who sinned against his Maker, and for whose sin the marks of the crucifixion are borne upon the Savior's form. As Adam sees those scars from the cruel nails, he does not fall upon the bosom of his Lord, but in humiliation casts himself at Christ's feet crying, 'Worthy, worthy is the Lamb that was slain!'"

Can you imagine this huge man, twelve to fifteen feet tall, casting himself down at Jesus' feet? (We had a big guy in college who went out to sell religious books one summer. Unfortunately, he was as bashful as he was tall. Later, he sheepishly told us what happened when he knocked at the first house. The lady opened the door and invited him in. Smiling, he stepped forward—and tripped across the door sill, falling flat on his face at her feet! We laughed and laughed as we pictured his plight.) But, what a different scene when Adam, the father of our race, chooses to fall at the feet of Jesus. Tenderly the Savior will lift him up and bid him look once more on the Eden home from which he has so long been separated.

Remember, after his expulsion from Eden, Adam's life on earth was filled with sorrow. Every dying leaf, every victim of sacrifice, every blight upon the fair face of nature, every stain upon man's purity was a fresh reminder of his sin. His agony was terrible as he saw iniquity abound. Imagine his remorse, when in answer to his earnest pleas and warnings he was reproached as the cause of it all. With patient humility he bore, for nearly a thousand years, the penalty of his transgression. Faithfully he repented, and trusting in the merits of the promised Savior, he died in the hope of a resurrection.

Now, the Son of God has redeemed man's failure, and Adam is reinstated in his first dominion. Transported with joy, he will behold trees that were once his delight—the very trees whose fruit he himself had gathered in the days of his innocence and joy. He will see vines that his own hands trained, the very flowers that he once loved to care for. As his mind grasps the reality of the scene; he will comprehend that this is indeed Eden restored, more lovely now than when he was banished from it.

As the Savior leads him to the tree of life and plucks the glorious fruit for him to eat, Adam will look around and see a multitude of his family, redeemed and standing in Paradise. He'll cast his glittering crown at Jesus' feet and embrace his Redeemer in love. Then he'll lift up his voice, and the vaults of heaven will echo with triumphant song. And Adam's family will join him, casting their crowns at the Savior's feet as they bow before Him in adoration.

This reunion is witnessed by angels who wept at the fall of Adam and rejoiced when Jesus (after His resurrection) ascended to heaven. Now, as they behold the work of redemption accomplished, they unite their voices in a song of praise...in the land where song was born! Can you imagine the glorious strains?

As we imagine this scene, I guess the only thing that *really* counts is *will you be there?* That's the bottom line. Are you spending time, day by day, becoming closer and closer to Jesus? The time is soon coming when the things of this world will look like trivia (or even less). Isn't it wonderful that Jesus has made it possible for us to join that heavenly throng?

Chapter Nineteen

Asking QUESTIONS

Are you going to be happy when you get to heaven? Not so fast! There's a difference between being happy *to get* there, and being happy *when* we get there. You've heard the song, "When we all get to heaven, what a day of rejoicing that will be. When we all see Jesus, we'll sing and shout the victory." But, there's another song that says, "I dreamed I searched heaven for you."

There are going to be some big surprises, and without doubt some tears, in heaven. People might be there we were sure *wouldn't* be. (We might find they didn't expect to see *us* there, either!) Or worse yet, we may be looking forward to being reunited with someone, only to find that they chose the other path.

Suppose you get to heaven and then realize that your next door neighbor is Adolf Hitler! You might wonder, "Am I in the right place?" You look out the window, and sure enough, there are the streets of gold. So rushing out of your mansion, you stop the first angel passing by and say, "I've got a problem. Is it all right to ask a question?" But the angel responds, "No, don't ask any questions here. Don't you trust God? The Lord knows those who are His." So you swallow hard, and for the next million years or so you bite your lip and try hard not to ask any questions.

Well, maybe you could learn to live with this unusual next door neighbor, but what about this: suppose you get to heaven and find your son or daughter is missing—then you discover the one who led them away from God and down the dark path to destruction lives just across the street! Now it's getting closer to home. You rush into the street and stop the first passing angel, and say, "Is it all right to ask questions here?" And the angel responds, "Yes! We want you to ask questions. We want you to understand." That's better, isn't it? Heaven is not a place where people forever serve God like mindless robots. Last I checked, they're going to serve God as intelligent creatures—and God will treat them as such!

So it makes sense to take a look at the post-advent judgment, when everyone appears in court (we're going to have jury duty, if you please). And the purpose of this courtroom scene is to help intelligent creatures understand the final judgements from God's perspective. This will take place during the thousand years of Revelation 20, which is also known as the millennium. (The word "millennium" doesn't show up in the Bible, but "thousand years" does. And the *only* place it appears is Revelation 20.)

The Millennium

Now, there's a big difference between the popular view of the millennium, and the millennium that's discussed in Scripture. We need to be quite clear on this.

The popular view of the millennium had its beginnings during the counter-reformation, when the Jesuits were trying to take the heat off the Papacy. Then in the last century, some people (who supposedly were Bible scholars) further modified this Jesuit interpretation of prophecy and began promoting their own adaptation. Today many Christians (from most denominations) believe this twice-modified concept, thinking that it comes from Scripture. (Remember, don't believe *anything* until you study it out yourself!)

But not everyone bought into the idea. Here's what pioneer radio evangelist, H.M.S. Richards, Sr. had to say over fifty years ago in a large church in Washington D.C., "There's a great difference between the Bible statement and the popular view of the millennium. Let me just pass this word along to you. The prevailing idea today about the millennial reign of Christ is that He will come secretly and catch away His church. That's called the secret rapture. Then after three and a half years some strange man will appear somewhere, the Jewish people will accept him as their Messiah and will be greatly deceived, because he's really the anti-Christ. After three and a half more years, he reveals himself to them with great cruelty. And to save the Jews, Jesus Christ comes in glory, sets up a kingdom at Jerusalem and reigns on earth a thousand years. The Jews go forth to preach the gospel. At the end of the thousand years, the devil comes forth and they have a big fight. Then the world explodes and they all go off to heaven." He got a little folksy there at the end, but Richards and serious Bible scholars like him were appalled at the general acceptance of a scenario not based on Scripture. Should we be less concerned today?

The primary difference between this view and Scripture is that the popular view has the millennium taking place *on earth*—and the "second chance" idea is woven all through the concept. Also, the beginning and ending points are not understood at all.

Here's what actually happens, according to Scripture. "For the Lord himself will come down from heaven, with a loud command, with the voice of the archangel and with the trumpet call of God, and the dead in Christ will rise first. After that, we who are still alive and are left will be caught up with them in the clouds to meet the Lord in the air. And so we will be with the Lord forever." (1 Thessalonians 4:16,17) The millennium *begins* with the second coming of Christ and the first resurrection, when all the righteous go off *to heaven* with the Lord.

What about everyone else? Jesus' second coming has no effect on the wicked dead; they remain asleep (see Revelation 20:5). And the unrighteous who are alive when Jesus comes are destroyed by the brightness of His coming. A thousand years pass, then the millennium *ends* at the third coming of Christ and the second resurrection (which raises all the unrighteous dead).

Well, if the wicked are all dead, and the righteous are all in heaven, then who's left on earth during the thousand years? Is it completely depopulated and uninhabited? Not quite. The fallen angels are still stuck here—as is their leader, Satan.

A Key Chapter

Which brings us to Revelation 20, where we find a clear outline of the thousand years. I've often wondered why some evangelists leave out the millennium. And why do so many of our "last day" books and seminars close with the second coming? There are BIG events that follow this, including the thousand years in heaven, and the final showdown at the end of the millennium. And although some of these scenes are scary, we shouldn't just ignore them!

(Now, I'm aware some people don't like the idea of God burning up the wicked. Some try to explain away the fire as simply symbolic. Some say that the righteous will ask God, before the thousand years end, to just let the wicked keep on sleeping. I've heard lots of these "improvements." But the *real* question is, do we trust God's word?)

Let's begin with Revelation 20:1-3: "And I saw an angel coming down out of heaven, having the key to the Abyss and holding in his hand a great chain. He seized the dragon, that ancient serpent, who is the devil, or Satan, and bound him for a thousand years. He threw him into the Abyss, and locked and sealed it over him, to keep him from deceiving the nations anymore..." (Where are the nations? Gone! A chain of circumstances binds the devil, including a depopulated earth—no one to deceive anymore! Apparently the abyss or pit the devil is confined to is the ravaged remains of our planet.) "..to keep him from deceiving the nations any more until the thousand years were ended. After that, he must be set free for a short time." Remember, the wicked come back to life at the end of the thousand years, so once again there are people to deceive. And Satan goes back to work.

What about the righteous in heaven during this thousand years? "I saw thrones on which were seated those who had been given authority to judge." Who are they? "...I saw the souls of those who had been beheaded because of their testimony for Jesus and because of the word of God." These are the martyrs back from their graves. But there's also another group, those who "...had not worshiped the beast or his image and had not received his mark on their foreheads or their hands." These are the people who've gone through the events we've been studying. "They came to life and reigned with Christ a thousand years. The rest of the dead did not come to life until the thousand years were ended..." (Revelation 20:4, 5).

Then comes a text (verse 6) that was ingrained on my mind as a boy. I'd sit on the ground at my dad's evangelistic tent meetings and make airplanes in the sawdust. But before I'd begin, I'd look up at the two banners hanging up front—two great Bible texts. "What shall it profit a man, if he shall gain the whole world and lose his own soul?" And "Blessed and holy is he that hath part in the first resurrection: on such the second death hath no power." That made a big impression on a little kid—and I've been grateful for it ever since.

Verse seven continues the story: "When the thousand years are over, Satan will be released from his prison and will go out to deceive the nations in the four corners of the earth—Gog and Magog—to gather them for battle. In number they are like the sand on the seashore. They marched across the breadth of the earth and surrounded the camp of God's people, the city he loves..."

Do you get the picture? After the second coming of Christ, all the righteous are in heaven; all the wicked are on earth—dead! The devil and his angels are left with three hundred sixty-five thousand days in the cemetery. And Satan is the sexton in charge. He's been much too busy in the past to pause and reflect, but now he has plenty of time! Imagine—centuries of thinking about where he came from, what he's become, and all the misery he's responsible for. If I were the devil, I think I'd commit suicide after the first week of the millennium. But he can't even do that!

During this time (between the first and the second resurrection) God's people are living and reigning with Christ, and the post-advent judgment of the wicked is taking place. (Obviously the judgment of the righteous is finished *before* the second coming. Some of us believe it began in 1844, in fulfillment of that long time prophecy of Daniel 8.) Then, as the thousand years end, the Holy City comes down from heaven with all the righteous inside. And all the wicked are raised. The righteous are inside the city looking out; the wicked are outside looking in. (We'll save the rest for the next chapter.)

Aspects of Judgment

Now, in order to better understand God's character, let's examine four aspects of His judgment on sin and sinners.

First, Romans 3:26 makes it clear that because of Jesus (and the judgment at the cross), God can be just and the justifier of those who believe in Him. As you know, God operates His universe on certain eternal principles. One of these is: "The wages of sin is death." (We're talking about the second death, not the one we call death.) You and I, as guilty sinners, the offspring of generations of sinners, would have no choice but death. But someone came and took our place. Because of Jesus, God can be just and forgive anybody. He can forgive *everybody*. It makes no difference who you are, where you've been, or what you've done. Everyone who comes to Jesus is always accepted and forgiven, and stands before God as though they'd never sinned.

However, this forgiveness that's provided, this justifying grace, is no good to anybody until they *accept* it. When I accept what Jesus did for me (and accept Him as my Savior, Lord, and Friend), my name is written in the book of life—and if I stay with Him, I'll stand among those who meet Jesus in peace when He comes.

By the way, the Bible doesn't teach "once saved, always saved." It teaches that *two* things are important: *coming* to Christ and *staying in a relationship* with Christ. That's why I like what my Nazarene friends told me. "We believe in once saved, always saved—as long as you *keep* saved." And how do you keep saved? You keep coming to Him, day by day, accepting anew His grace. Notice, our personal, daily relationship with Christ is not what saves us—but it *is* the way that we continue to accept His saving grace!

Point number two: The second aspect of judgment (the *pre*-advent judgment) makes it possible for God to be just and forgive those who are forgiven when He comes. It reveals those who have not only *accepted* Christ and His salvation, but have also *continued* to accept His grace.

Point number three: The third aspect of judgment (the *post*-advent judgment) makes it possible for God to be just and to *not* forgive the ones who *aren't* forgiven. It's all bound up in one awesome idea—that God, Himself, is willing to be judged. He's willing for the universe, and everyone who's ever lived or died, to look at how He has worked, and see if He's been fair and just from the very beginning.

Let's review what we have thus far. First, the judgment at the cross made it possible for God to be just and to forgive anybody. Second, the pre-advent judgment allows God to be just and forgive the ones who have accepted and continued to accept Him. And third, the post-advent judgment shows how God can be just and not forgive those who aren't forgiven.

And, there's also a fourth aspect of judgment that we call "the judgment of the great white throne." (We'll take a look at that in the next chapter, too.)

More on Judging

During the thousand years, the judgment of the wicked takes place. The Apostle Paul points to this judgment as an event that follows the second advent. "Therefore judge nothing before the appointed time; wait till the Lord comes. He will bring to light what is hidden in darkness and will expose the motives of men's hearts." 1 Corinthians 4:5 Notice there are two parts here: God shows what's been going on in the dark, *and* He shows people's motives for their actions.

That's why *we* can't judge anybody. Only God knows what makes people tick. And that's why we have to realize that man looks only at the outward appearance, but God looks...where? At the heart! We're going to have the opportunity during the thousand years, painful as it might be, to face what's been going on in the dark, and understand what's been going on in people's hearts.

My son tells a story that tears me apart. He was a beginning teacher in a Colorado high school. One morning, just as school was about to begin, a girl pulled up in front of the administration building and parked in the wrong place. As she got out of her car and came rushing through the door, the vice-principal came out of her office and pointed out the parking error. This teen turned on the vice-principal and said, "I don't need you! Don't tell me what to do. I'm sick and tired of people telling me where to park and what to do!" And she continued screaming while the administrator just stood there with her mouth open. Then the girl turned and ran down the hall into class. My boy saw it happen. A lot of students heard it, too. And my son frowned and thought, "What a way to run a school!"

Well, she was in one of his classes. So he began to make a point from then on, whenever she was even a moment tardy, to mark her down. And whenever it was grading time and she was close to the line, he never gave her the benefit of the doubt. He didn't cut her any slack at all. And soon, school was over for that year.

During the summer, the faculty of this private school sat down to review student applications for the following year. As the list was read, any teacher who had doubts about a name raised their hand. If three faculty members' hands went up, then the student's name was placed on a list for further consideration. They came to this girl's name. My son raised his hand—but nobody else did! They were about to go on to the next name, when my boy interrupted. "Wait a minute," he said. "You don't understand. This girl has an attitude problem!" And he proceeded to tell what he'd seen that day. There was a moment of silence, then the vice-principal said, "Well, maybe I should speak to this." She said, "I remember that experience. Thirty minutes after she exploded, I went to the classroom and asked her to come to my office. Then I said to her, 'The way you reacted this morning makes me think there's something else bothering you. Want to talk about it?' She began to cry and the story bubbled out. That morning she'd stood for a long time listening to her parents (who were in the process of divorce), screaming and yelling at each other. Finally, she saw she wasn't going to make it to school on time, so she interrupted—a big mistake! Her father turned on her and verbally tore her to ribbons. He condemned her for ever getting born, and said he didn't need her around! Well, she finally managed to find some car keys and got to school by herself. Then she was confronted with the parking problem. It was just too much for one day."

My son felt like crawling in a hole, and he's been telling that story ever since to try to convince people we'd better stop judging!

There's an interesting principle here: God looks not only at *what* we do, He looks at *why* we do it. Aren't you glad for that? But it works both ways, you know! Let's exaggerate this to the extreme: Suppose in the heavenly judgment we find out that Billy Graham didn't make it, but Adolf Hitler did! Billy Graham spent years and years in evangelism only because he was on a big ego trip; and Adolf Hitler had struggles we never knew about, and in that bunker that night he turned his life over to God. (Pretty far fetched, isn't it—but you get my point.) Only God knows the *real* truth. Only *God* knows!

Jury Duty in Heaven

John says, "I saw thrones, and they sat upon them, and judgment was given unto them...they shall be priests of God and of Christ, and shall reign with Him a thousand years." (Revelation 20:4,6) Paul also foretold that the saints would judge the world. In union with Christ they will judge the wicked, comparing their acts with Scriptural statutes, and deciding every case according to the deeds done. Satan and his evil angels are also judged by Christ and His people.

Do you have problems with this scene? I've known people who are ready to hang their doubts on this. (You can always find room to doubt, even in God's inspired Word. Some say, "I'm not interested in Christianity because the Bible contradicts itself. One gospel writer says Jesus came *into* Jericho as he healed the blind man; another says He was *leaving*." So, they give up heaven and the resurrection and eternal life over trivia. How foolish can you get?) Some think they have a case in the millennium. They say, "What loving Christian could tolerate a thousand years of true confession magazines?" (I've heard people wallow in their own intellect with this type of approach.) Others say, "Well, if this is what we're to do during the millennium, I'm going to cry for a thousand years!" (Tears in heaven? Revelation 21 talks about tears being wiped away in the New Earth after the millennium, so there must have first been some tears in heaven.)

What's the problem with these approaches? They don't seem to recognize the nature of our God! *God loves us.* Isn't it possible our jury duty won't last any longer each day than we can handle? Maybe God will let us practice our "touch and goes" on the Sea of Glass during the off hours. And children probably won't do jury duty at all. Scripture says the streets of the city shall be filled with boys and girls playing. (Zechariah 8:5). Boys and girls in heaven? Yes, maybe even brand-new babies! God plans incredible joys for His people.

There will also be the marriage supper of the Lamb in heaven. (Revelation 19.) As a part of the Lamb's bride, we're all invited.

There's a table, miles and miles long (maybe you can't even see the end of it), filled with food. And as we sit down to eat at this wedding feast, Jesus Himself will be serving. That's the way He is, always serving. "Would you like to try a helping of this, my child? What about another serving of that?" And if He sees us weeping, He'll bring out His heavenly handkerchief and gently dry our eyes. That's because Jesus is there to serve, and He loves us.

In heaven, maybe Adam will need a little help trimming those vines in that garden he's thrilled to be in again. We don't know the details of what it will be like—but we do know one thing. Somewhere in the picture will be a group of people singing a song of praise to God with all their hearts. They're not going to sing because the heavenly angels have twisted their arms behind their backs. They're not going to sing because they are programmed into it, or they feel a sense of duty. They'll burst forth with song because it's an intelligent admission of what they really feel—in spite of any pain and heartache.

And when this time is over, our hearts will beat in unison with the heart of God forever. For God has been willing to put Himself on the line to be judged.

In Our Place

Let's close this chapter by going back to the pre-advent judgment for a moment. (I surely don't want you to review *my* records in the *post*-advent judgment!)

Now I used to have trouble with the pre-advent judgment. Somewhere I got the idea that during this time the angels would get out their heavenly adding machines and add up all our good deeds and all our bad deeds. If we have more good deeds than bad deeds, then we make it! And I was certainly happy my name was down at the bottom of the alphabet, so I'd have just a little more time!

But then it finally dawned on me. If we accept Christ (and keep accepting Him), then we don't even come *into* the judgment. (see John 5:24).

Picture this for a moment. Somewhere before Jesus comes back the second time, my name comes up for judgment: Morris Venden. Now, I'm in big trouble! But then there's someone, the best Friend I've ever had, who goes in my place. A voice says, "Where is Venden?" And Jesus says, "I'm here to represent him. He's my friend! I told him he didn't have to be here today." Incredible! I'd like to be somewhere in the bleachers when Jesus takes my place in the judgment. (But since I can't, then during the millennium I'd like to check out that video and watch it...and watch it...and watch it!)

And those whose hearts beat with the heart of Jesus will forever sing His praise. "And I saw what looked like a sea of glass mixed with fire and, standing beside the sea, those who had been victorious over the beast and his image..." Remember, the victory they've gotten is the victory of no longer living their lives *apart* from Jesus. That's *the* victory! And they sing "the song of Moses, the servant of God, and the song of the Lamb: 'Great and marvelous are your deeds, Lord God Almighty. Just and true are your ways, King of the ages.'" (Revelation 15:2,3) And they mean it! They've had a chance to look through God's eyes.

You say there are still some hard questions about the thousand years, about the end of the thousand years, and about the destruction of the wicked—things you don't completely understand? I agree. We're using limited human minds to try to understand heavenly things. We must ask God to make clear those things we need to know, and learn to trust Him for the rest. After all, don't we already have enough evidence of His love and His fairness because of the cross? Shouldn't we be able to trust Him, knowing whatever He does will be right?

In the end, it all boils down to this one question: "Are you willing, are you anxious, to totally trust in God?"

Chapter Twenty

When Everyone MEETS...

Is the final end of the wicked a big barbecue party? That was the question a smart guy asked several years ago when we were at a large church in Los Angeles. He'd been reading Revelation 20 and raised serious questions as to whether a God of love would throw a barbecue to end things. In the process, I'm sure he managed to raise enough doubts in some people's minds that they forgot all about the rest of the things in the Bible—including heaven and eternal life and peace and joy and the resurrection.

Friend, if you're doubting God in any way because of the means He'll use to bring a final end to the sin problem, then you have a bigger issue to settle first regarding God's character.

That said, let's take a look at the events that take place at the end of the thousand years. As you recall, the first resurrection takes place at the beginning of the thousand years—the righteous are raised from the dead (and meet the Lord in the air). Then there's a thousand years in heaven, when all the righteous serve jury duty, and the streets of the city are filled with boys and girls playing. We've also noticed other things going on, like the marriage supper of the Lamb, and maybe even a few "touch and goes" on the Sea of Glass.

At the end of the thousand years the second resurrection, the resurrection of the wicked, takes place. And Satan is let out of prison. (He and his angels have been confined on this depopulated earth and forced to think about what they've done—365 thousand days in the cemetery.) Revelation 20 says the devil and his angels and all who have come up in the second resurrection "marched across the breadth of the earth and surrounded the camp of God's people, the city he loves. But fire came down from heaven and devoured them. And the devil, who deceived them was thrown into the lake of burning sulfur..."

The Holy City Descends

And now, we enter the grand finale in the great controversy between Christ and Satan. As the Holy City descends from heaven, Satan begins to marshal his troops. Scriptural clues indicate that the city will hover above the Mount of Olives (which will flatten out and become a plain), waiting for the final great showdown. Since the righteous were raised in the first resurrection, and all the wicked in the second, now is the time when everyone who has ever lived meets for the first and last time. Millions of people are on the inside of the city looking out, millions more are on the outside looking in.

Those who've come up in the second resurrection are deceived by the enemy into thinking that *he* has raised them from the dead, and that he's their savior! But they come forth from the grave the same way they went in—maimed, and crippled, and diseased. You wonder how they can even survive in that condition! But apparently the enemy is permitted to give them a shot of adrenaline or something, and he convinces them that they can overpower the city by force of numbers, and still win the great controversy.

Now let's take a look at their target, this "City of God". According to the dimensions in Revelation 20, it's about the size of Oregon! That's one big city! But is it big enough for the millions of redeemed?

We'd probably each have only a few square feet to stand on. So this city's construction must be different than cities we're used to.

Scripture says the Holy City is as high as it is wide. And there's even evidence (check the foundation structure) that it occupies more than three dimensions! From those twelve foundations, sections of such a city would be reaching out in every direction. An awesome, spectacular sight, this architectural marvel that descends from heaven is the governmental capital of the universe.

But, on his side, the enemy has people from all the ages, including generals who've never lost a battle. And he convinces them that they can surround this mighty city and overthrow its King. So the great showdown begins.

Inside the city are people who've gone through everything that people on the outside have gone through. In fact, I believe there'll be an honor guard, because God needs people who can be trusted. For everyone on the outside who's gone through hard times, and shook their fist at God and shouted, "You can have your heaven and eternal life", there'll be someone on the inside who went through the same experience, and who remained true to God.

The Last Conflict Begins

So these two groups meet for the first and last time—let's take it from there and try to imagine what it might be like:

The order is given to advance, and the countless host starts toward the city—an army unlike any ever summoned by earthly conquerors. The combined military forces of all the ages since war began could not equal it. Satan, that mightiest of warriors, leads the host. Kings and warriors are in his army, and multitudes follow in vast companies. Even Satan's angels join in this final struggle. With military precision the massive ranks advance over the earth's broken, uneven surface toward the City of God. (Perhaps they've had time to reassemble the same resources that tore the earth apart earlier, including thermonuclear devices and all that goes with them.) Jesus commands the gates of the New Jerusalem to be closed, and the armies of Satan surround the city and make ready for the attack.

But now, in the presence of the assembled inhabitants of earth and heaven, the final coronation of the Son of God takes place. Far above the city, on a foundation of burnished gold, a throne is lifted up. On it sits the Son of God, in full view of His enemies. His power and majesty are beyond description. The glory of the Eternal Father enshrouds Him. The brightness of His presence fills the Holy City, flowing out of its gates, and flooding the earth with radiance.

Around Him are the subjects of His kingdom. Near the throne stand those once zealous in Satan's cause, but now, "plucked as brands from the burning", they follow their Savior with deep, intense devotion. Beside them are others whose characters were perfected in the midst of falsehood and infidelity, and millions from all ages who were martyred for their faith. And, before the throne and before the Lamb is that "great multitude which no man could number" of all nations, kindred, tongues, and peoples clothed with white robes, the emblems of the spotless righteousness of Christ that is now theirs.

Salvation to Our God

The redeemed now begin to sing a song of praise that echoes and re-echoes through heaven: "Salvation to our God who sits upon the throne, and unto the Lamb." Salvation *to* our God?! Aren't they making a big mistake? Isn't that supposed to be salvation *from* our God? No, it's *God's* salvation at stake here. It's *His* reputation being put on the line. And apparently that's one of the primary reasons that everyone who has ever lived is in that final audience.

The redeemed have seen the power and awfulness of Satan, and they realize, as never before, that no power but Christ's could have made them conquerors. In all that shining throng, no one ascribes salvation to themselves; not one believes they prevailed through their own power or goodness. And no one talks of what they've done or suffered. Some of them were torn apart on the rack; some ripped to pieces by lions; some slowly reduced to ashes at the stake. Others in this group, like Paul, were beaten and left for dead. But they're not thinking about what *they've* been through. The entire focus is on Jesus and salvation to our God and to the Lamb.

As the loving eye of Jesus looks on the wicked with sorrow, they become conscious of every sin they've ever committed. They see just where their feet diverged from the path of purity and holiness, just how far their pride and rebellion have carried them. The seductive temptations they encouraged by indulging in sin, the blessings perverted, the warnings rejected, the waves of mercy beaten back by stubborn, unrepentant hearts—all these are in the minds of the lost.

Then comes the most incredible video (or full screen presentation) you can imagine. God's audio-visual department makes Disney's Epcott Center look like nothing. Every eye inside and outside the city is riveted to the three hundred and sixty degree, wrap-around screen, high above the throne of God.

Every detail of the great controversy is now replayed, just as it happened, from beginning to end. (Who knows how long it will take—days, weeks? And does it really matter, since time no longer has any meaning?) Everyone stands transfixed by this great video in the sky. In panoramic view appear the scenes of Adam's temptation and fall; the successive steps in the great plan of redemption; the Savior's lowly birth; His early life of simplicity and obedience; His baptism in Jordan; the fast and temptation in the wilderness; His public ministry, unfolding to men heaven's most precious blessings; the days crowded with deeds of love and mercy; the nights of prayer and watching in the solitude of the mountains; the plottings of envy, hate, and malice which repaid His benefits; the awful, mysterious agony in Gethsemane beneath the crushing weight of the whole world's sins; His betrayal into the hands of the murderous mob; the fearful events of that night of horror; the unresisting prisoner, forsaken by His loved disciples, dragged through the streets of Jerusalem; the Son of God arraigned in the high priest's palace, then in the judgment hall of Pilate, then before the cowardly and cruel Herod—mocked, insulted, tortured, and condemned to die. Everything is vividly portrayed.

And now the final scenes are revealed to the swaying multitude. The patient Sufferer treading the path to Calvary; the Prince of heaven hanging upon the cross; the haughty priests and the jeering rabble deriding His expiring agony; the supernatural darkness; the heaving earth, the rent rocks, the open graves, marking the moment when the world's Redeemer yielded up His life. The awful spectacle appears exactly as it happened.

Satan, his angels, and his subjects would turn from the picture, but they have not the power. Each recalls the part which he performed. Herod, who slew the innocent children of Bethlehem that he might destroy the King of Israel; the base Herodias, upon whose guilty soul rests the blood of John the Baptist; the weak, political Pilate; the mocking soldiers; the priests and rulers and maddened throng who cried, 'His blood be on us, and on our children!'—all behold the enormity of their guilt. They seek to hide from the divine majesty of His countenance, outshining the glory of the sun, while the redeemed cast their crowns at the Savior's feet, exclaiming: "He died for me!"

(Notice the difference between people on the inside and those on the outside. The redeemed cry, "He died for me!" and rush to be near Him. The wicked look for some place to hide.)

Among the ransomed are Christ's apostles: the heroic Paul, the ardent Peter, the loving John, and a vast host of martyrs. But outside the walls, with every vile and abominable thing, are the very ones who persecuted, imprisoned, and slew them. Nero, that monster of cruelty and vice, beholds the exaltation of those he once tortured, in whose anguish he found satanic delight. His mother witnesses the results of her own work; how the evil character transmitted to her son, the passions encouraged and developed by her influence, bore fruit in crimes that made the world shudder. Papist priests and prelates are there; men who claimed to be Christ's ambassadors, yet employed the rack, the dungeon, and the stake to force the conscience of others. The whole wicked world stands arraigned at the bar of God on the charge of high treason against heaven. Through their own choice, they have no one to plead their cause; they are without excuse.

Now, forgive me for this next statement—I'm not trying to be mean, only thoughtful. Among the crowds out there with Nero and Hitler and the rest of the wicked, there's the church member who went to church from habit, and wouldn't think of doing anything wrong—but who had no time for Jesus. He chose playing over praying. He preferred football to Jesus. Will he be angry at God? You bet! Listen to him shout, "What am I doing out here with Nero and Hitler? I never did anything wrong!" Do you follow what's happening here?

Every Knee Shall Bow

As if in a trance, the wicked have watched the coronation of the Son of God. They've witnessed the outburst of wonder, rapture, and adoration from the saved. And now, as the wave of melody sweeps over the walls, all with one voice exclaim, "Great and marvelous are Thy works, Lord God Almighty; just and true are Thy ways, Thou King of saints"; and falling prostrate, they worship the Prince of life.

Notice, this happens on both sides of the wall—inside and out! Here's another reason why everyone who's ever lived is together one final time. It was predicted long ago that (by their own choice) every knee would bow, and every tongue confess that God is fair.

What about Satan? The devil seems paralyzed as he beholds the glory and majesty of Christ. He was created "Lucifer"—a shining seraph, the "son of the morning." Now he is Satan; horribly changed, and forever degraded! From councils where he once was honored, he is forever excluded. Another stands in his place near the Father, veiling the Father's glory. Satan sees this angel of lofty stature and majestic presence (whose name is Gabriel) place the crown on the head of Christ, and he knows this angel's exalted position might have been his. He remembers his earlier life in heaven, the home of his innocence and purity. He recalls the peace and contentment that were his, until he indulged in murmuring against God and envy of Christ. His accusations, his rebellion, his deceptions to gain the sympathy and support of the angels, his stubborn persistence in making no effort for recovery when God would have granted him forgiveness—all these things come vividly before him.

And Satan also reviews his work among men and its results. He has seen the enmity of man toward his fellow man; the terrible destruction of life; the rise and fall of kingdoms; the overturning of thrones; the long succession of tumults, conflicts, and revolutions. He recalls his constant efforts to oppose the work of Christ and to sink man lower and lower. As Satan looks upon his kingdom, the fruit of his toil, he sees only failure and ruin. He knows his hellish plots have been powerless to destroy those who have put their trust in Jesus. He has led the multitudes to believe that the City of God would be an easy prey, but he knows this is false. Again and again, in the progress of the great controversy, he has been defeated and compelled to yield. He knows too well the power and majesty of the Eternal.

Satan also sees that his rebellion has made him unfit for heaven. He has perverted his powers in the war against God. Purity, peace, and the harmony of heaven would be, to him, supreme torture.

And now Satan's accusations against the mercy and justice of God are stilled. The reproach he has endeavored to cast upon Jehovah rests wholly upon himself. And Satan bows down to confess the justice of his sentence. "Who will not fear you, O Lord, and bring glory to your name? For you alone are holy. All nations will come and worship before you, for your righteous acts have been revealed." (Revelation 15:3) Can you imagine this scene?

The Final Battle

But even though Satan has voluntarily acknowledged God's justice and has bowed to the supremacy of Christ, his character remains unchanged. Suddenly, like a mighty torrent, the spirit of rebellion again bursts forth. Filled with frenzy, he determines not to yield. The time has come for his last desperate struggle against the King of heaven. He rushes into the midst of his subjects and endeavors to inspire them with his own fury, and arouse them to instant battle.

But of all the countless millions he has allured into rebellion, none now acknowledge his supremacy. His power is over. They simply stand and stare at him. And, as Isaiah prophesied, the millions on earth look at him and wonder, "Is this the one who made the earth tremble?" The wicked still are filled with the same hatred for God that inspires Satan (including church members who had no time for spiritual things), but they see that their case is hopeless and they can't prevail against God. So their rage is kindled against Satan, and those who have been his agents in deception, and with the fury of demons they turn upon them.

And now comes the greatest brawl this universe has ever seen! People tear at each other's throats, blaming and accusing, trying to rip each other limb from limb. But suddenly (mercifully) fire comes down from heaven. The earth is broken up. Weapons concealed in its depths are drawn forth, and devouring flames burst from every yawning chasm. The very rocks are on fire. The day has come that shall burn as an oven. The elements will melt with fervent heat and the works of the earth will be burned up. The planet's surface seems one molten mass—a vast, seething lake of fire. In the cleansing flames the wicked are at last destroyed, root and branch (Satan the root, his followers the branches). "All the arrogant and every evildoer will be stubble, and that day...will set them on fire...not a root or a branch will be left..." (Malachi 4:1). The full penalty of the law has been visited, the demands of justice have been met, and all heaven beholds the scene, declaring the righteousness of Jehovah.

Theories of Destruction

Over the years, a lot of people have been troubled by the final destruction of the wicked—and so several theories have sprung up regarding this time. I'll describe them, then you can take your pick.

First, we have the "universal salvation" theory. The people who subscribe to this theory believe that *everyone* will ultimately be saved, even the wicked. They think that even the devil and his angels will probably be converted and will join the church. (I've got news for them—I think the devil joined the church a long time ago!)

Then there's the "deeper understanding" theory. It's based on the idea that the millennium is designed to increase the insight and compassion of the righteous. They'll watch all the videos, and gain a deeper understanding of the "big picture." (Perhaps you've heard the *results* of a famous trial and wondered how they came up with their verdict. But in this case, you'll be on the jury.) Then, the righteous will come to God, and say, "Lord, we understand now how bad sin is, so you can call off the second resurrection. Just leave the wicked in the grave and we'll be happy." So much for that version.

There's also the "symbolic language" version. This theory says that all those fire and brimstone words in Scripture are merely symbolic. This interpretation is an attempt to get God off the hook; to portray a nice God who never hurts anybody. "Fire symbolizes love," they say, "and people suffer because of His love, not because He tortures them." And this view has been quite popular in recent times.

It's interesting that those who want to keep God from appearing mean are often the very same people who will admit that the mental torture of the wicked is much more painful than the fire. But then, that brings up another question. "Isn't God responsible for *this*?" "Oh no," they say, "they're responsible for their own mental torture! No one can be blamed for having lit any flames." But, wait. Didn't God raise them from the dead in the second resurrection—which is why they're around to experience this mental torture in the first place? (We're getting into rather deep waters here!) And something else to remember. Many raised in the second resurrection were among those at Christ's return who begged the rocks and mountains to fall and hide them. They wanted to die. (I suppose there's also the question of which is worse, to have El Capitan fall on you or to be burned up.)

There's another version of the theory that the fire is symbolic. It says that people who are lost will one by one go through extreme mental anguish, and finally admit that God was right and they were wrong. Their stubborn resistance gradually fades away until they say, "O.K. I give up." Then, having lost their will to live, they die. And it takes different people different amounts of time to reach this point, including Satan (who takes the longest of all). Then the literal fire simply comes along and cleans up the debris.

And finally, there's the "mercy killing" theory. It begins with the idea that perhaps we don't fully understand what the second death is all about. Some have said, "The thing that tortures the wicked at the end is that they see they're going to be separated from God forever." Come on! There's nothing they'd like better! That's why they wanted the rocks and mountains to fall on them. For them, it would be *heaven* to be separated from God forever. No, the second death, apparently involves something much more than mere separation.

Let me give you an example. A man called me one day and said, "I've been to hell and back." He'd lost everything that previous year—his high-paying executive position, his house, his car, his family, and almost his mind. So one day he got mad at God, and essentially said,

"If this is the way you're going to treat me, you can stick it in your ear." He cursed God and shouted, "I don't want any more to do with you. Get out of my life!" And God, apparently answered his prayer. For three days, he told me, he was in hell. "I've never understood what the second death is going to be like until now," he said. "The despair, and the abandonment, and the absolute sense of nothingness were overwhelming!"

And as I listened, something began to dawn on me. Apparently God supplies the "will to live" that we need just to function—even if we use it to go to Las Vegas to gamble! Without the presence and power of God in our lives (even among the wicked), we wouldn't be able to do *anything*—except vegetate in utter helplessness, hopelessness, and abandonment. Mental torture? Apparently it's beyond anything we've ever imagined! Not because God causes it (even though He raises the dead to face it), but because that's the way it is apart from God.

A Question of Trust

Well, shall we take a vote? Which of these versions do you prefer? In order to put it all in perspective, let me ask you another question instead. Are you willing to allow for God's vindication, and this clue that we picked up earlier—salvation to our God? No matter *how* the wicked are destroyed, something about this last great showdown is necessary and important to the universe. And that is the assurance that sin will never rise up again.

Coupled with that question is an even more important one: *Do you trust God?* As I said earlier, if one chapter in God's Word causes you to get discouraged and give up on the rest of His book (and abandon your faith), then you've got bigger problems.

So what if one Gospel writer says Zacchaeus climbed a Sycamore tree, and another says it was a fig tree? Is that enough to make you say, "That's it. Goodbye salvation! No more heaven, no eternal life, no resurrection, no more joy..." Friend, if that's all it takes to undermine your faith, then you've got a much deeper issue to deal with. Do you follow me at all? If you're looking for an excuse to hang your doubts on, you'll definitely find one. (And the devil will help you in your search since it serves his ends!)

Once again, the *real* question is, "Do you trust God to know what He's doing in this last showdown—*however* it ends? Are you willing to totally and completely *trust* Him?"

"But," you say, "there are still some awfully big mysteries!" Yes, that's true. And that's why it meant so much to me one day (after I'd been struggling with some of these same questions) when my father offered a suggestion. He said, "Son, here's just one sentence from an inspired pen that might help you: "The mystery of the cross explains all other mysteries." Wow!

Purifying Fire

Are you interested in "going for the gold"? There's a spectacular city with streets made of gold that makes the majesty of the Olympics look like peanuts. Don't you want to be there when the fire has finally burned out and the saints of God get to watch Jesus create the earth all over again? "Then I saw a new heaven and a new earth, for the first heaven and the first earth had passed away..." (Revelation 21:1)

The fire that consumes the wicked purifies the earth. Every trace of the curse is swept away. There's no "eternally-burning hell" to keep before the ransomed the fearful consequences of sin. Only one reminder of sin will remain forever. Jesus will always bear the marks of His crucifixion. The scars on His wounded head, on His side, and on His hands and feet are the only traces of the cruel work of sin. Does that mean we'll see those scars forever? Apparently yes. And each time we do, we'll be overwhelmed with loving gratitude.

The New Earth

Originally, the earth was given to man as his kingdom. But through sin, Adam betrayed the planet into the hands of Satan, and through the centuries it's been held in the cruel grip of this mighty foe.

But now the earth has been bought back by the blood of Christ—and the earth will be made new! The great plan of redemption has restored all that was lost by sin. And the glorious reward of the righteous defies human comprehension. The beauty and fulfillment of living in paradise is completely beyond our finite minds—it's an experience to be fully understood only by those who live it.

Scripture calls the inheritance of the saved a "country." And what a country it will be! Ever-flowing streams, clear as crystal, flow beside waving trees that cast their shadows on winding pathways. Wide-spreading plains swell into hills of beauty, and the mountains of God rear their lofty summits. And on those peaceful plains, beside those living streams, God's people (for so long pilgrims and wanderers) shall find their homes.

One day, as a boy, I stood beside the Columbia River with my father as he showed me the house that his father had built. Many people have lived there since. He showed me the apple trees that they'd planted when he was a kid. Scores of people have eaten those apples since then.

But it won't be like that in the heavenly country. "They will build houses and dwell in them; they will plant vineyards and eat their fruit. No longer will they build houses and others live in them, or plant and others eat...my chosen ones will long enjoy the works of their hands." (Isaiah 65:21,22) There "the desert and the parched land will be glad; the wilderness will rejoice and blossom...it will burst into bloom." (Isaiah 35:1,2), and "The wolf will live with the lamb, the leopard will lie down with the goat, the calf and the lion and the yearling together; and a little child will lead them." (Isaiah 11:6)

(A little child shall lead them? That ought to wake you up. This is *after* the millennium, in the new earth, and "a little child will lead them". Put that in your computer!)

Pain cannot exist in the atmosphere of heaven. There will be no more tears, no more funerals, no more times of grief. "He will wipe every tear from their eyes. There will be no more death or mourning or crying or pain, for the old order of things has passed away." (Revelation 21:4) "No one living in Zion will say, 'I am ill'; and the sins of those who dwell there will be forgiven." (Isaiah 33:24)

There the redeemed shall know, even as they are known. The loves and sympathies which God Himself has planted in our souls shall find their truest and sweetest exercise there. No longer will a cruel, deceiving enemy tempt us to forget God. Our immortal minds will contemplate with never-failing delight the wonders of creative power and the mysteries of redeeming love. Our every faculty will be fully developed, every capacity increased. Acquiring new knowledge will not weary our minds or exhaust our energies. In the new earth, the grandest enterprises may be carried forward, the loftiest aspirations reached, the highest ambitions realized—and still there will be new heights to climb, new wonders to admire, new truths to comprehend, and fresh objects to call forth the expanding power of our minds, our souls, and our bodies.

And all the treasures of the universe will be open for our study. Unfettered by mortality, God's people will wing their tireless flight to worlds afar—worlds that shuddered with sorrow at the spectacle of human woe, and rang with songs of gladness at the tidings of a ransomed soul.

The day will come when your guardian angel (with whom you've become the best of friends) says, "Let's go on a trip." "Where to?" you ask. "To a far country; a little planet on the outer rim of the universe. The inhabitants want to hear from human lips what it's like to be redeemed from a world of sin." So you say, "If you'll help me, I'll go." And you do—even though you're not a public speaker any more than Moses was. And the angel gathers that group together, and blessed with power and courage, you speak of your Savior.

And although I'm not an angel, I know in that heavenly country I'll sing like one! And I'll join the redeemed in a chorus that even the angels cannot sing:

> "I will sing about my Savior,
> Who upon dark Calvary
> Freely pardoned my transgression;
> Died to set a sinner free.
> Holy, holy is what the angels sing,
> And I expect to help them make
> The courts of heaven ring.
> But, when I sing redemption's story
> They will fold their wings.
> For angels never felt the joy
> That our salvation brings."[1]

[1] Johnson Oatman, Jr.

Chapter Twenty-One

The TROLLEY

They never noticed it at first, for as they approached the trolley car, the conductor had called out, "Careful, watch your step!" So they focused on being careful and watching their step. Then there was the confusion and bustle as everyone looked for a good seat, and decided who to sit next to, and whether to sit by a window or on the aisle. After that, they were talking back and forth and getting acquainted with their fellow passengers (many of whom had been on board some time already). And then the conductor had come around to collect the fares.

But finally someone noticed. "This trolley car isn't moving!" they said. Everyone looked out the window, and sure enough—the trolley was sitting still! No one was sure exactly how long ago it had stopped. In fact, it appeared to be sitting right where they'd gotten on. There were exclamations all around of "See that little cafe? That's where I had breakfast before I boarded." And "I remember that big brick building down the street."

The conductor tried to calm the passengers. "We'll get there, just be patient. These things take time." Someone called out, "Exactly when are we supposed to arrive at our destination?" "Well," replied the conductor, "No one knows the exact day or hour. Some say we'd have been there long before now, if there hadn't been delays. But one thing I can tell you for sure—if you'll just be patient and stay with this trolley car, you'll get there."

Time passed slowly, then suddenly a large man jumped to his feet. "I think it's about time we figured out why this trolley isn't moving," he said. "Let's have a committee meeting and discuss ways and means for getting it going again." Everyone was in favor of that, so they elected the large man as chairman (since it was his idea to have a committee in the first place).

"Mr. Chairman," said a man near the front, "I think we're still here because the fares are too high. How can we make any progress when the conductor keeps coming around asking for money all the time?"

"That's a good point," an energetic young man interrupted. "But what we really need is to get some more passengers on this car. Look at all the empty seats! If we had passengers to fill this trolley to its full capacity, we'd have *much* more money."

An older, distinquished-looking woman raised her hand. "With all due respect to the views thus far expressed," she said, nodding toward the last speaker, "quantity is not the problem. We do not need quantity, but *quality*. I move that we get rid of some passengers, keeping only the better class of society. When this trolley becomes known for the high quality of its passengers, we'll be on our way."

Everyone secretly thought this was a great idea and immediately thought of several people they'd like to see put off. But then they wondered if someone might nominate *them* for removal, so no one would vote for it, and the suggestion was "tabled for futher study."

Then the chairman had an idea. "Why don't we redecorate the trolley?" Everyone agreed immediately, and it looked like progress was finally being made—until they began to discuss what color scheme to use. Part of the passengers wanted blue carpeting and upholstery, but the rest wanted red. Arguments were loud and long over the point, and the interior decorating committee died a slow and angry death.

Shortly after this, an idea surfaced that almost everyone liked.

Someone suggested that the real problem was the conductor, and that what they needed to get the trolley moving again was to fire him, and get a new one. The idea quickly caught on. The passengers were finally united in a common goal, and it wasn't long until the conductor was gone and a new face appeared. But they didn't like the new conductor any better than the last one. (He was always asking for money, too!) And the trolley car still wasn't moving.

Every so often someone would say, "I'm tired of this trolley car never going anywhere. It's never gone anywhere and it never will! I'm getting off." And whenever that happened, the conductor and the rest of the passengers would try to encourage these restless ones by reminding them that this was the "only true trolley", and that if they'd simply be patient, they'd surely arrive at the destination. If that didn't work, they'd get one of the older passengers (who'd been on board for a long, long time) to tell of past experiences.

You see, all along the road to the Destination were signs. Most of the passengers couldn't personally remember seeing any signs (except the one right outside the spot where the trolley was sitting that said, "destination, straight ahead.") But some of the older passengers could remember a time when the trolley was still moving, and they'd seen one sign after another. Back in those days the trolley had been clipping right along, and it had been thrilling to see a sign which said, "Destination, Far Ahead," and then later another sign, "Destination, Lots Closer Now." Some of these older passengers had become so excited about watching for signs that they always sat in the very front of the trolley car, eyes strained, watching for the next signpost. And these older passenger would join the conductor in encouraging the other passengers to keep watching. After all, they were almost there. Any time now they would move ahead just enough to see that last sign saying, "Destination, City Limits"—and the trip would be over.

Well all of this went on for much longer than it takes to tell. Then one day a rather quiet, unassuming passenger was stretching out an open window and happened to look up. High above the trolley was an electric cable, and attached to the top of the trolley was a connecting device. But the trolley wasn't connected to the cable. Greatly excited, the passenger stuck his head back inside the window. "Hey you people! I think I've discovered something! We're not connected up above—we're not connected to the power source! Maybe that's why we're not moving!"

But the committee, deep in a discussion about whether or not it was appropriate for passengers to wear blue jeans on the trolley, hardly heard him.

Undaunted, he continued to shout. "Listen!" he exclaimed. "We're not connected to the power! No wonder this car doesn't move—come on and look for yourselves. There's equipment to connect, but we just aren't connected!"

A few other passengers came over to the windows and joined him leaning out and looking up. Sure enough, they *weren't* connected to the power overhead. Amazed, this small group began to earnestly discuss how they could become connected to the source of power. Eagerly, they began to read The Trolley Car Manual and to carefully follow its directions. Soon others joined them, and the excitement continued to build.

There were some passengers, of course, who strongly opposed these actions and called them fanatical. But in spite of opposition, the time came when the majority of the passengers understood for themselves about the source of power, and what was needed to make the connection. With their encouragement, the stalled trolley was once again attached to the power source, and with a shudder and a groan, it at last began to move.

But suddenly, a most amazing thing happened! The passengers who didn't agree with "connecting to the power source" were so terrified when the trolley actually began to move that they began leaping out of the windows, right and left! And as the trolley began to pick up speed, all their ideas about this trolley being "the only true trolley" were hastily discarded, and they rushed off to find another trolley that wasn't moving—so they could continue their committee meetings in peace!

And what happened to the trolley car that was moving? Well, the last I heard, it was getting very close to the final Destination.

End Time EVENTS

45 Theses from Scripture on Last Day Events

The Close of the Great Controversy between Christ and Satan

1. Laodicean Message .... Revelation 3:14-20
2. Preparing for the Crisis .... Matthew 7:24-27
3. Revival and Reformation .... Psalms 85:6; Isaiah 57:15
4. Early Rain of the Holy Spirit .... Joel 2:23
5. Satan's Delusions .... Matthew 24:23-26
6. False Revival... Matthew 7:21-23
7. Secret Rapture and "Futurism" .... Matthew 24:23-27
8. Spiritism (the Occult) ....Revelation 16:14
9. The Shaking .... Revelation 3:14-20
10. The Sealing .... Revelation 7:1-8
11. Remnant (Church) ....Revelation 12:17; 14:12
12. 144,000 plus Great Multitude .... Revelation 7
13. The Three Frogs .... Revelation 16:12-16
14. Global Crisis ....Revelation 11:18
15. The Loud Cry .... Revelation 18:1-4

16. Latter Rain of Holy Spirit .... Acts 2:17,18; Zechariah 10:1

17. Witness before Rulers .... Matthew 10:16-19

18. The Image of the Beast .... Revelation 13:14,15

19. The Mark of the Beast .... Revelation 13:16,17

20. Religious Legislation .... Revelation 13:16,17

21. Leaving the Cities .... Matthew 24:15-16, 20-21

22. Early Time of Trouble .... Matthew 24:9-13

23. Persecution .... Luke 21:12; II Timothy 3:12

24. Sifting .... Mark 4:17; Matthew 13:21, Amos 9:9

25. Courage of the Martyrs .... Matthew 10:28

26. Close of Probation .... Revelation 22:11,12

27. Without an Intercessor .... Daniel 12:1

28. Four Winds Released .... Revelation 7:1-3

29. Great Time of Trouble .... Daniel 12:1

30. The Seven Last Plagues .... Revelation 15:1; Revelation 16

31. Counterfeit Second Coming .... II Cor. 11:14; II Thes. 2

32. Death Decree ....Revelation 13:15

33. Leaving for the Mountains .... Isaiah 33:15-17

45 Theses on Last Day Events (cont. from p. 227)

34. Time of Jacob's Trouble .... Jeremiah 30:3-7

35. Battle of Armageddon .... Revelation 16:12-16

36. God's People Delivered .... Daniel 12:1; Isaiah 25:9

37. Special Resurrection .... Daniel 12:2

38. Second Coming of Christ .... I Thessalonians 4:16,17

39. Resurrection of Righteous .... I Thessalonians 4:16,17

40. One Thousand Years .... Revelation 20:1-10

41. Third Coming of Christ .... Revelation 21:2,3

42. Resurrection of the Wicked .... Revelation 20:5-6

43. Last Confrontation .... Revelation 20:7-9

44. Satan, Sin, Sinners no more .... Revelation 20:9

45. New Heaven and New Earth .... Revelation 21:1-5

Author's Understanding of End Time Events

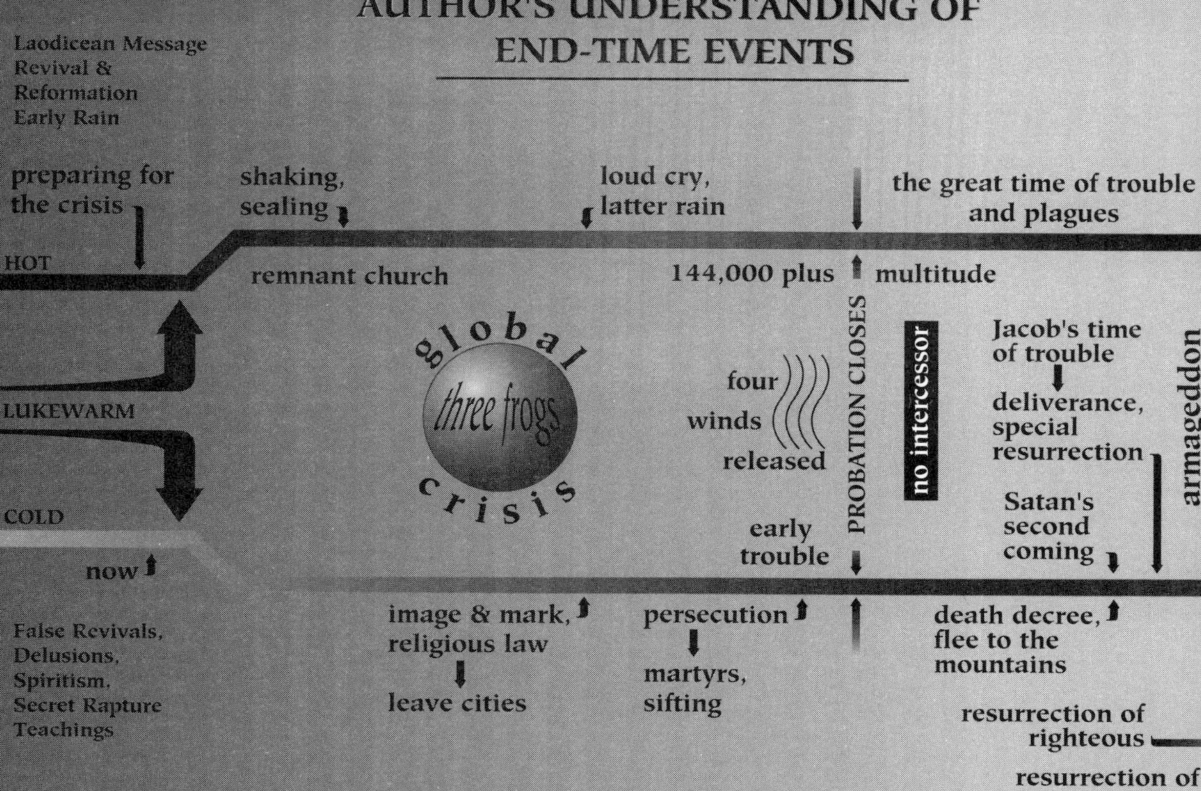

AUTHOR'S UNDERSTANDING OF
END-TIME EVENTS
Laodicean Message
Revival &
Reformation
Early Rain
preparing for
the crisis
shaking,
sealing
loud cry,
latter rain
the great time of trouble
and plagues
HOT
remnant church
144,000 plus
multitude
LUKEWARM
COLD
global
three frogs
crisis
four
winds
released
PROBATION CLOSES
no intercessor
Jacob's time
of trouble
deliverance,
special
resurrection
Satan's
second
coming
armageddon
early
trouble
now
False Revivals,
Delusions,
Spiritism,
Secret Rapture
Teachings
image & mark,
religious law
leave cities
persecution
martyrs,
sifting
death decree,
flee to the
mountains
resurrection of
righteous
resurrection of
wicked
SECOND COMING
all righteous
in Heaven
1000
years
all wicked
dead on
earth
Satan bound
THIRD COMING
earth
made
new
no
more
sin

Vintage
Publications